HEALING
CHAKRAS

HEALING CHAKRAS

Awaken Your Body's Energy System
for Complete Health, Happiness, and Peace

ILCHI LEE

BEST
LIFE

BEST LIFE

BEST Life Media
6560 Hwy. 179, Suite 114
Sedona, AZ 86351
www.bestlifemedia.com 1-877-504-1106

This book should be regarded as a reference source and is not intended
to replace professional medical advice. Seek the advice of your physician
before beginning this or any other health program. The author and the
publisher disclaim any liability arising directly or indirectly from the use
of this book.

First paperback edition: 2005
Second paperback edition: 2009
ISBN-13: 978-1-935127-04-8

Cover design: James Bennett
Illustrations: Al Choi, Kyoung Hwa Park

If you are unable to order this book from your local bookseller, you may
order through www.bestlifemedia.com.

Printed in South Korea

The part can never be well unless the whole is well.
—*Plato*

Contents

Introduction Finding the Right Balance in Life 10

Part I The Seven Chakras 17

What Are Chakras? 18
First Chakra   : The Jade Gate 22
Second Chakra : The Earth Palace 26
Third Chakra   : The Sun Lotus 30
Fourth Chakra : The Mind Palace 34
Fifth Chakra   : The Soul's Gate 38
Sixth Chakra   : Heaven's Palace 42
Seventh Chakra : Heaven's Gate 46

Part II Energetic Anatomy 53

The Three Bodies 54
Chakras and the Body and Brain 57
Activating the Chakras as They Relate to the Brain 59
Light, Sound, and Vibration 62

Part III Chakras and Your Spiritual Development 65

The Secret Tradition of Chakra Healing   66
Secrets of Heavenly Transformation of Shin-sun-do 71
Living for the Growth of the Soul 74

Chakras and the Heavenly Code 76

Chun-Bu-Kyung, the Heavenly Code 78
The Principle of Creation and Evolution 80
The Principle of Water Up, Fire Down 82
The Principle of the Light and the True Self 84
The Principle of the Oneness of the Cosmic Self 85
The Principle of Eternal Life 86

The Chakras and the Completion of the Soul 87

The Three Gates 87
The Three Palaces 89
The Three Births 90
Healing Chakras and the Soul 91

Part IV Healing Chakras Exercises 95

Chakra Relaxation 96

Self-Observation 98
Energy Sensitivity Training 99
Energy Dance 103

Feeling Your Chakras 104

Locating the Chakras in Your Body 104
First Chakra   : Hwe-um 106
Second Chakra : Dahn-jon 108
Third Chakra   : Joong-wahn 110
Fourth Chakra : Dahn-joong 112

Contents

Fifth Chakra   : Cheon-dol 114
Sixth Chakra   : In-dang 116
Seventh Chakra : Baek-hwe 118

Activating the Chakras with Vibration   120
Beginning Vibration Training 122
Chakra Vibration Training 124
Concluding Chakra Vibration Training 127
Vocal Chakra Healing 128

Strengthening the Chakras   132
Making an Energy Glove 134
Generating a Capsule of Energy 137
Strengthening the Energy Capsule 139

Healing the Chakras   143
Shower of Light 145
Transmitting Energy with Your Hands 148

Partner Healing   150
Sensing the Energy Field of a Partner 150
Placing an Energy Capsule on Your Partner 151

Chakra Meditation   154
Listening to the Message of the Soul 155
Pure Consciousness Meditation 158

Part V Living a Healthy Chakra Lifestyle 161

Chakra Color Meditation   162
First Chakra   : Light of Passion 165
Second Chakra : Light of Creation 166
Third Chakra   : Light of Life 167
Fourth Chakra : Light of Love 168
Fifth Chakra   : Light of Peace 169
Sixth Chakra   : Light of Wisdom 170
Seventh Chakra : Light of Completion 171

Exercises to Awaken the Chakras   172
First Chakra   : Strength, Courage, and Decisiveness 172
Second Chakra : Creativity 174
Third Chakra   : Inner will and Creativity 176
Fourth Chakra : Relief from Anxiety and Nervousness 178
Fifth Chakra   : Emotional Control and Inner Peace 180
Sixth Chakra   : Intuition, Inspiration, and Insight 182
Seventh Chakra : Oneness with the Cosmos 184

Index 186
About Ilchi Lee 190
Guide to Healing Chakras Self-Training CD 192

Finding the Right Balance in Life

I assume you picked up this book because you are interested in chakras. Well, let me set the record straight. This is really a book about happiness.

Chakras would have no interest for me whatsoever if they were just some esoteric spiritual concept. The only thing that interests me is helping people create better lives for themselves. To that end, chakras are really just a practical matter. You cannot live a truly happy life if your energetic condition is not in a healthy state. My hope is that the information in this book will help you achieve just that.

The seeds of Healing Chakras training were actually planted over thirty years ago on a mountain top in Korea. It was at that time, when I was in my early thirties, that I underwent my own deep training experience. For years, I had been searching for the answers to some of the fundamental questions of human existence. I kept desperately asking myself, "Who am I? Why am I here?" I would not be satisfied with conventional ideas about personal identity. I had to know, really *know*, what this life was all about. Thus, I went up into the mountain, determined to not come down until I found the answer. I didn't even care if I were to die in the attempt.

Fortunately, I did find the answer—after twenty-one days of grueling ascetic training. The answer came to me like a thunderbolt to my brain, just at the moment I thought I would die up there in the mountain. While deeply meditating on a rock on the edge of a cliff, I suddenly felt as though my head were going to explode, and electricity was coursing through my body. I thought, "This is it. I am going to die here," as I imagined myself tumbling over the edge of the cliff.

But I did not die. Instead I heard a voice in my head saying, "Cosmic energy is my energy; my energy is cosmic energy." At that moment, I felt as though my entire being was dissolving into the energetic soup of the universe. Feeling my existence as pure energy, I felt without any doubt that all separations are illusionary, and that all is one through cosmic energy. With this realization came an incredible sense of peace and bliss. Since that moment, it has been my mission to help people open themselves to this enlightenment experience.

I have identified the brain as the ultimate mediator in this enlightenment process because it is only through the brain that people can experience oneness, just as it is the brain that creates our illusions of separation. Thus, for the past thirty years, I have been constantly working to create training methods that help develop the brain's hidden abilities and sensitivities. These methods, collectively called Brain Education System Training (BEST), are now taught in more than 1,000 centers around the world, as well as in numerous schools and community centers.

Much of the BEST system is an expanded and modernized version of the training practices that were part of the Korean Shin-sun-do tradition, the original Korean culture of more than

10,000 years ago. Ruled by enlightened figures known as the *Dahn-guns*, this society was one of the most peaceful, advanced cultures ever to have existed. For them, energy study was a normal part of everyday life. I believe that this ability to sense and connect to energy was a key element of their enlightened culture, and I believe energy study can do the same for people today, which is why I have written *Healing Chakras* for you.

I consider Healing Chakras training to be an important part of BEST because understanding of and sensitivity to energy is the key to health, happiness, and peace. One unique aspect of this Chakra program is how it is connected to the human brain, which is ultimately the mediator for the health of the entire chakra system.

In 1999, I first started a training called Energy Capsule Training, and two years later developed it into Healing Chakras training, the one you will experience through this book. From 2001 to 2003, I traveled around the United States, Canada, United Kingdom, Korea, and Japan to present Healing Chakras. I conducted about ninety trainings and met some 15,000 people through this training. Starting in 2004, I selected very advanced students of mine to give Healing Chakras training. Since its inception, about 30,000 people have experienced Healing Chakra training through 300 sessions.

Much of what you will read and experience through this book is related to the Healing Chakras lecture and training workshops.

Healing Chakras training is a four-hour intensive workshop. You can feel, activate, and balance all seven chakras through the training, which emphasizes the spiritual aspects of chakras and restores a strong connection between the human and the divine. Many wonderful stories of healing and personal transformation have resulted from this training. While there are many chakra books on the market today, you can rest assured that the exercises contained within this book have worked for real people, making their lives more healthy, happy, and peaceful.

This book is based on the notion that energetic health is the foundation of mental, physical, and spiritual health, what I call "health, happiness, and peace." As far as I am concerned, asking, "Are you well?" is akin to asking, "Are your chakras healthy?" Energy is the root of body and mind. By understanding and mastering energy, you can unlock the secret to changing yourself and the world. When a chakra changes, energy changes. When energy changes, personal transformation is achieved.

Thus, by learning to pay attention to your energetic health, you are learning to look deeply at the underlying causes behind any physical ailment or mental discomfort you may have. As you will discover, the various chakras represent different aspects of human existence. To a great degree, healing your chakras is about finding the right balances in life.

Ultimately, however, I believe that Healing Chakras is about healing the Earth. The imbalances we see in the world today are a keen reflection of the imbalances people have in their bodies, minds, and spirits. By learning to feel and understand your own chakras, you will bolster your connection to other people and to the Earth. Divisions will disappear. As we heal ourselves, we heal each other and the Earth.

Ilchi Lee
Sedona, AZ
July 2009

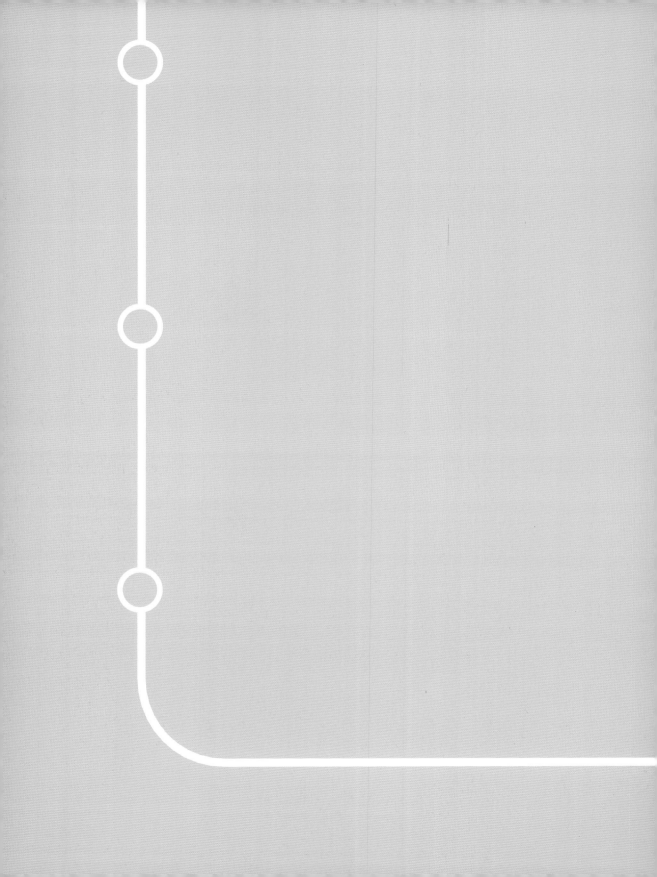

Part I
The Seven Chakras

What Are Chakras?

Have you ever thought of yourself as an energetic being? Actually, everything you are is ultimately energy. Yes, your body may seem solid to the touch, but really, when you get right down to it, you are nothing but energy. Your body is composed of cells, which are composed of atoms. And what are those atoms made of? Energy.

Many ancient traditions speak to us of a different kind of energy, a kind of life energy, that runs through all living things. In the Asian traditions, this form of energy is called *chi*, *qui*, or *ki*. The whole system of Asian medicine, including acupuncture, is based on an intuitive understanding of how ki works in the body. According to this system, energy runs through a network of pathways in the body that are called "energy meridians." When a practitioner of Asian medicine works to heal, he or she works to identify and remove any blockage to the flow of energy in the body.

Essentially, *chakras* are energy centers in the body. A chakra is like Grand Central Station, a hub in which the energies of mind, body, and spirit are intertwined and sent through the meridians for use in our daily life. You might think of chakras as outlets of cosmic energy, allowing our energy bodies to plug into the universal power source. Running down the midline of the body, there are seven of these energy centers, located on the crown of the head, the forehead, the throat, the chest, the upper abdomen, the lower abdomen, and the genital area. When these seven chakras are functioning well, we are healthy in body, mind, and spirit.

Each chakra governs a specific kind of energy related to various human attributes. For example, the heart chakra is the domain of the mind and the emotions. If the heart chakra is functioning well, the person will demonstrate emotions in a constructive way and will be open to others around him or her. The tendency to close oneself off from others or to be dominated by emotions suggests some problem in that energy center. When unhealthy, a chakra can be either under- or over-stimulated. The key for any of the chakras is balance.

Overall, the chakra system is related to our individual growth and development of consciousness. The lower chakras deal with more primal issues of survival, sexuality and power, while the upper chakras are concerned with issues of personal expression, insight, and spiritual completion. In theory, as we progress through life, we will progress up the chakra system, beginning with the first chakra in infancy and developing the upper chakras as we mature into adulthood. In reality, however, this process is rarely without interruption. The process of living and growing presents us with certain difficulties, and thus many of the chakras may require extra effort to maintain energetic balance.

It is important to note that while the chakra system does reflect the upward growth of human consciousness, all chakras remain important to the individual's overall state of health. You should not think, for example, that development of the sixth

chakra, the center of insight and intuition, is somehow more important than development of the second, the center of physical strength and power. In fact, the development of the second chakra is an important foundational step for the development of the sixth. If the sixth is developed without proper attention to the second, the individual may exhibit an ungrounded and ineffective form of spirituality.

It is not an overstatement to say that complete health begins and ends with the chakras. Problems with the chakras are rooted in problems of the body, mind, and spirit. A change in the chakras signifies transformation of the truest sort.

The Jade Gate

1ST Chakra

Planted deeply in fertile soil

The flower of life blossoms forth

Providing strength

On which to feed and prosper

Gate through which we enter the world

Announcing our arrival on Earth

The first chakra is the seat of the unconscious mind, housing the instinctual drives for food, sex, and survival. Through the first chakra life is brought into being, preserved, and reproduced. You entered into this world through your parents' first chakra, as they were brought into being through *their* parents' first chakra. All future generations will also be brought forth through the first chakra.

It is through the first chakra that we experience our natural sense of self-preservation. A person with a healthy first chakra possesses a natural love of life and a basic love of self. Good habits of self-care, such as cleanliness, good nutrition, and regular exercise, are motivated by a healthy first chakra. While a person with a healthy first chakra proactively ensures his or her own safety and well-being, he or she also has a natural trust in the abundance of life, knowing that basic needs will be provided for. The first chakra can inspire a sense of confidence and trust for any aspect of life.

Generally, the first chakra develops in utero and during the first few months of life. If the infant's parents are not attentive or nurturing, or if the infant's environment is in some other way troubled, lifelong difficulties with the first chakra may develop. When the first chakra is underdeveloped, the individual may exhibit a nervous, insecure disposition. He or she may also have a poor body image or engage in self-destructive behaviors. By the same token, the first chakra may become overactive, resulting in greedy, self-obsessed behavior. The ultimate first chakra dysfunction is suicide.

Sexuality is a major issue for the first chakra. The first chakra may become blocked later in life if highly restricting attitudes about sex are embraced. Overactivity of the first chakra may also lead to sexual addiction or unsafe sexual habits.

Certain aspects of modern society can make it difficult to keep the first chakra healthy. Negative information and fear-based thinking are like a disease to the first chakra, creating a culture of overconsumption and greed. Society's conflicting and unhealthy attitudes about sexuality further complicate the matter. For overall health and happiness, the first chakra must be healthy to serve as a foundation upon which all other chakras may be built.

. . . .

The color of the first chakra is deep red, the color of blood and the color of passion. A seed, sparked with the energy of life, represents the forces of nature that bring life into being. Surrounding the seed are waves of the ocean of life, the primordial birthplace of all living things.

. . . .

The Earth Palace

2ND Chakra

Earth Palace, nurturing the seed of the physical body

With the rich energy of the belly ablaze

Water energy goes up, and fire energy comes down

In accordance with the harmonious order of life

The second chakra is like the boiler room of the body's energy system. From this chakra we gain the power to go forth into the world with proactive confidence. It is through this chakra that we can anchor ourselves to the Earth and to the center of our own being, allowing us to remain strong in the face of turmoil and strife. When this chakra is on fire with abundant life energy, our bodies easily maintain their equilibrium and health.

If you have ever felt the "fire in the belly," you have felt the second chakra. The second chakra is like the engine of the body, providing the power to move forward in life. For overall physical health, this is perhaps the most important of the chakras, as it provides a feeling of strength and wellness.

The second chakra helps govern the hot and cold energies of the body. In Asian medicine, there is a concept called "water up, fire down." It refers to the fact that, when in balance, the body demonstrates a very predictable pattern of circulation of energy. As the phrase suggests, when we are healthy cool water energy should rise in the body, cooling the brain. Heat energy, on the other hand, should remain low in the body. When we are healthy, both mentally and physically, we keep a "cool head" and a warm abdomen. The first chakra, when strong, helps to regulate this process.

Health of the second chakra is indicated by overall robust health, as well as physical strength and endurance. When the second chakra is fully activated, you will literally feel it as heat in the lower abdomen. An underdeveloped second chakra, by contrast, can result in weakness, fatigue, and disease.

Although emotions do not emanate from the second chakra, it does play an important role in regulating the mind's emotions, which are rooted in the experiences of the physical body. The second chakra can serve as a kind of anchor for the easily fluctuating fourth chakra, which regulates the emotions. The second chakra is literally in the very center of the body, and thus, when developed, can provide an unshakable sense of grounding and centeredness.

The second chakra can be developed through physical exercise, especially the kind that develops endurance. A sedentary lifestyle is very bad for the second chakra, leaving people physically weak, emotionally wavering, and prone to disease. A strong second chakra is the key to a strong body, mind, and spirit.

· ·

The color of the second chakra is red orange, reminiscent of fire. In the center of the chakra there is an exploding volcano, representing the powerful force of the physical body. A dragon rises from the volcano, representing life energy as it rises up from the second chakra, up the spine, and to the entire body, filling it with life. A square represents the planet Earth, to which we connect through the second chakra.

· ·

The Sun Lotus

3RD Chakra

In pink and yellow glory

A lotus flower in the solar plexus

Loving, eating, drinking, working, living

Master of the desire for life

Shining brightly within those who seek a beautiful life

It is from the third chakra that our will and our desire for life emerge. The energy from this chakra propels us forward toward the fulfillment of our dreams and goals. When this chakra is fully activated, we are keenly aware of our life's purpose and are able to continuously orient ourselves in that direction.

The third chakra governs one of the most important human attributes—creativity. Even if you do not view yourself as creative, you have tremendous creative ability. Some of us manifest this creativity through art and music, while others apply their creativity to developing a business or creating a great home life. In actuality, you are creating in every moment with every choice you make and every action you take. Thus, your third chakra is a vital governing force in your life.

One important aspect of creativity is will, which is also governed by the third chakra. Before you can do or make anything in the world, you must first have sufficient will to make it happen. In this sense, the third chakra is the motivator of the sixth chakra, which is the seat of our intellect. The intellect may have some intention or inspiration for your life, but if the third chakra is blocked, it will be hard to carry it to fruition. Many people have a lot of great ideas and many grand dreams, but, because their third chakra is blocked, they have difficulty bringing these things into the physical world.

Blockage in the third chakra often results from unresolved issues in regard to authority and empowerment, also governed by the third chakra. Sometimes, outside authority, in the form of leaders and laws, do block us from creating what we want. But more often than not, our internal sense of authority is a bigger issue than external authority figures.

Many people block their creative power through their own beliefs about themselves. Here again, the sixth chakra is interacting with the third as the intellect produces disempowering thoughts that block the sixth. Believing themselves unworthy or unable to create what they want in life, their third chakra remains black and their dreams remain unfulfilled. Creating a solid sense of empowerment and internal authority is thus very important for the health of the third chakra.

By the same token, the third chakra can also become overactive. This results in a highly aggressive approach to self-creation and a lack of concern for the needs of others. In this case, the sense of self-empowerment and personal authority has gone awry. Overwork and obsession with status and material success are also dysfunctions of the third chakra.

The best way to ensure the health of the third chakra is to develop a strong personal identity rooted in your higher self. Through a strong identity, you will always be able to strike the right balance between personal empowerment and compassion.

The color of the third chakra is orange, like the sun, the ultimate energy source powering all life on Earth. The moon is also shown in all of its phases, representing creative power, changeability, and transformation. It reflects the growth of the individual human throughout life, as well as the constantly changing, cyclical aspect of all nature.

The Mind Palace
4TH Chakra

Mind Palace, seat of the soul

Golden lotus, shimmering

Love and compassion residing within

Giving rise to honesty, diligence, responsibility

Coming together with dignity

The fourth chakra is our heart chakra, whose health dependant upon the health of our thoughts and emotions. With this energy center wide open, we face the world with an open mind and a loving heart. It is also from here that we can grow the flower of a beautiful character; it is the foundation of personal integrity and ethical conduct. Through this chakra, we can also connect and commune with the hearts and minds of others on this earthly path.

The fourth chakra is like a golden rose that must bloom and open fully during your life. The seat of the emotional mind, it is through the fourth chakra that we can experience some of the most joyous aspects of life. When fully open, the fourth chakra sends out rays of loving energy that can touch anyone in our immediate environment.

While the previous three chakras relate primarily to the physical body, the fourth is the first to take us beyond the limits of our personal self. From here we can begin to reach out beyond the egoic mind to experience connection and oneness with others. This can be difficult, as we experience the emotional hurts that are part of the process, but the rewards of doing so are great.

The fourth chakra is the seat of all emotional experience, both positive and negative. While it is true that emotions can have a spiritual effect, emotions are the result of the limitations of the physical body. When we exceed our limitations, we feel joy and love; when we are confined by limitations, we feel anger and sadness. Yet, it is also through emotion that we can begin to develop the compassion that is the hallmark of our True Self.

Almost everyone will experience some sort of heart blockage at some point in their lives. It is the natural result of our individual needs and desires coming into conflict with those of others. This process can be painful, but it is only through this experience that we can break free of our limits, like a butterfly breaking free of the cocoon, to experience the beauty of our divinity.

Life is a constant process of opening and reopening the heart chakra. The fourth chakra is highly reactive, opening and closing according to our responses to the world around us. When we habitually build up walls that keep the heart shut away and protected, we fall victim to sadness, loneliness, and arrogance. In its most extreme state of dysfunction, the heart becomes overwhelmed by hate and bigotry, which may lead to violent actions in the world.

The key to keeping the fourth chakra open is positivity. While it is normal to react negatively to some circumstances, you can train yourself to be more and more accepting of your environment and to embrace differences in others. As you practice keeping your heart chakra open, differences will disappear and environments will be transformed before your eyes. When this happens, you will have glimpsed the power of your own divinity.

• •

The color of the fourth chakra is a bright golden yellow. Its bright, joyful light beams out to the world, spreading joy and love. The peach tree represents a paradise on Earth, a world full of beauty and love. The tree is laden with ripe peaches, a traditional symbol of enlightenment in Asian traditions. The cupped human hands represent the individual's openhearted receptivity to enlightenment, which begins with the opening of the fourth chakra. The triangle represents humanity.

• •

The Soul's Gate

5TH Chakra

Gate through which the soul travels

When the blue lotus blooms from the throat

Its azure light connects the Jade Gate

With Heaven's Gate

Allowing advancement of the soul

The fifth chakra is the bridge between the animal and the divine energies of the human being. Located in the throat, it is also the chakra that allows our expressive abilities. The quality of our speech, negative or positive, indicates the state of this chakra. The opening of this chakra allows the development of our divine aspect.

Everybody needs a voice. This is true externally, in relationships and in politics, and internally, as we develop our inner voice that guides us through life. Learning to develop, express, and listen to this voice brings your fifth chakra to full expression.

The voice allows us to express our divinity to the world. In fact, the negativity or positivity of our speech may be a primary indicator of our spiritual health. Also, it is through the voice that we can first learn to put our higher life purpose into reality in the physical world. When we express our desire and intention to make a difference in the world, we have made a huge step toward doing just that. It is also through our voice—through music, poetry, and oration—that we can touch the hearts of those around us and celebrate our common divinity.

If the fifth chakra is underdeveloped or blocked, a person may be shy and unable to express himself or herself clearly. Often, this is the result of self-judgment or the fear of judgment from others. Unfortunately, this lack of open communication only results in more problems that lead to more judgment and guilt. To overcome this, practice expressing your feelings and intentions to others without reservation. Also, work on developing clearly defined goals and intentions for your life so that you can express them well.

If the fifth chakra is overly active, the person may be loud, overly opinionated, and crass in his or her speech. The key to healing this chakra is the establishment of a clear sense of one's higher purpose and divine nature so that the voice becomes a platform for personal empowerment, but not for boastful speech. Speech that harms another's sense of divinity, such as cruel or hateful speech, is an indication of an individual's disconnection from divinity.

The fifth chakra is also considered to be the gate through which the second of three births occurs. The first birth, of course, is your physical birth into the material world. The third birth is your final birth after fulfillment, when you have completed your soul and return to the heavenly sphere. During your life, you must also pass through the gates of the chakras by giving full expression to your divine nature and purpose. Thus, spiritual development begins with the development of the fifth chakra.

The color of the fifth chakra is green, the color of growth, rebirth, and renewal. The butterfly in the center of the chakra represents transformation toward our second birth as spiritual beings. The staircase represents the constant, upward striving toward the expression of our True Selves and the path to completion. It also symbolizes the cervical vertebrae through which the energy of the fifth chakra rises up to the last two chakras.

Heaven's Palace

6TH Chakra

Heaven's Palace, source of the rhythm of life

When the indigo lotus appears within the mind's eye

It awakens the divinity within

Our second birth into a life whole and everlasting

The sixth chakra is the home of our spiritual and intuitive selves, connecting us to heaven's rich supply of wisdom and insight. This is the seat of both intellectual and spiritual development. With this chakra wide open, we can rise above the suffering of life to see the infinite wisdom that guides the universe.

The sixth chakra is often referred to as the "third eye" because it is a part of us that can indeed see, although on the spiritual rather than physical plane. Through the sixth chakra, we are able to see beyond the physical world into the greater reality of the cosmos.

If you have ever had a flash of insight into a difficult problem or a sudden intuitive feeling about something coming in the future, then you have experienced your sixth chakra. When activated, the sixth chakra provides a "knowingness" about realms of reality that are beyond the comprehension of the rational mind. When the third eye is completely open, many people exhibit psychic and telepathic abilities.

Another aspect of the sixth chakra is the intellect, which includes the imaginative and rational aspects of the mind. Through the rational mind, we can understand ourselves and the world better, and we can come up with solutions for problems in our daily lives. Imagination can help us visualize a better world and can entertain us with fanciful ones.

One should be careful not to get stuck in the delights of the intellect, however, since this is not everything the chakra has to offer. Sometimes people are so enamored of the rational mind that they neglect the development of the intuitive in favor of continual intellectual development. Most modern educational systems unfortunately promote the notion that useful knowledge is primarily gained through training of the rational mind combined with factual understanding.

The ultimate realities of life, though, cannot be discovered through the intellect. Often, one's rational mind fails to understand things beyond what is not obvious to the five senses of the body, thereby effectively blocking one's natural intuitive abilities. Thus, completely opening the sixth chakra requires stepping beyond the trap of the rational mind.

In today's world, many people possess a highly activated but partially closed sixth chakra. In the Information Age, most people receive information at an incredible rate of speed, and that information is continuously processed and evaluated by their rational minds. The third chakra becomes overloaded with information, which is very unhealthy for the mind and spirit. This condition can disrupt the "water up, fire down" energy balance, causing energy to pool in the location of the sixth chakra.

One important milestone for the sixth chakra is the perception of one's life purpose. You will know you have found this thing when you have found the activity that makes you happy mentally, emotionally, and spiritually. If your sixth chakra is open enough, you will know intuitively that you have found that thing. After discovering this life purpose, you can form a specific vision to fulfill this purpose.

• •

The color of the sixth chakra is blue, representing the heavenly the vastness of skies and oceans. The third eye, the source of intuition and divinity, peers forth from the center of the chakra. The eye floats in a field of clouds, which represent the heavenly sphere. Crystals represent the purification of humanity's divine aspect. The circle represents heaven.

• •

Heaven's Gate

7ᵀᴴ Chakra

Place of our third birth

A heavenly transformation

Violet lotus rising from the crown

Liberating your soul to absolute freedom

Completing your energy body

Communing with cosmic energy

It is through the seventh chakra that we reconnect to heaven, our original home. As we open this chakra, we open ourselves to oneness with all that exists. This is the center of the soul's completion and spiritual enlightenment. We pass through this gate into our final stage of our soul's journey, becoming one with a universal flow of cosmic energy.

The seventh chakra provides us with a direct energetic connection to heaven. This chakra will open completely when you complete your soul, and it is through this chakra that your soul will be returned to heaven one day. You can begin to open this chakra by realizing that you are a child of heaven who will one day leave the material plane to return to your celestial home.

In the *Chun-Bu-Kyung*, an ancient Korean spiritual document, much is expressed about the ultimate nature of humanity and our place in the universe. According to that text, the human being exists as part of a triad of heaven, Earth, and human. When the seventh chakra is open, we will be able to resume our position as intermediary between heaven and Earth, which is the ultimate purpose of enlightenment.

Just as we gain vital energy and Earth energy through the first chakra, we gain divine heavenly energy through the seventh chakra. Many of the problems in the world today can be seen as the result of disconnection from heaven, which can only happen through the seventh chakra. Many people feel a sense of futility in life because, with a closed seventh chakra, they can no longer feel the divine nature of their being. Also, when that connection it lost, focus is placed on material rather than spiritual pursuits, which leads to the greed and violence that plagues our planet.

Just as birth is an important event related to the first chakra, death is an important event for the seventh chakra. Upon the moment of death, the soul passes through this gate to achieve its third birth. If the soul is complete, the soul will join with the rest of heaven, becoming once again part of the undivided celestial sphere. If the soul is not complete (that is, fully enlightened and fulfilled), the soul will have to continue the cycle of incarnations as it is born through a yet another body to experience another journey through the three gates. This process will continue again and again until completion is achieved.

The color of the seventh chakra is purple, the color of the ultimate royalty—divinity. An infant sits in the middle of the chakra to represent our third and final birth, the completion of the soul. Hundreds of lotus petals surround the infant, representing the infinite, timeless nature of life beyond the body and beyond the ego.

	Shin-sun-do name	Acupressure Points	Common Name	Location	Color
7TH Chakra	Heaven's Gate	Baek-hwe	Crown	Crown of head	Purple
6TH Chakra	Heaven's Palace	In-dang	Third Eye	Forehead	Navy Blue
5TH Chakra	Soul's Gate	Chun-dol	Throat	Throat	Blue-green
4TH Chakra	Mind Palace	Dahn-joong	Heart	Sternum	Gold
3RD Chakra	Sun Lotus	Joong-wahn	Solar Plexus	Navel Area	Orange
2ND Chakra	Earth Palace	Dahn-jon	Sacral	Lower Abdomen	Soft Red
1ST Chakra	Jade Gate	Hwe-um	Root	Perineum	Dark Red

Function	Healthy	Unhealthy	Growth Stage
Connects to heaven	Wisdom, sense of oneness	Early senility, lack of inspiration	Completion of the Soul
Intuition and insight	Intelligence, wisdom, insight	Cynicism, lack of focus, headaches, eye problems	Recognition of divinity
Voice and expression	Verbal skills, effective communication	Shyness, inexpressiveness, depression, thyroid disease	Development of internal strength
Personal power, emotions and mind	Positive character and emotions, happiness	Emotional instability and repression, heart problems	Character development
Will and authority	Good digestion, achievement of goals	Lack of will, fear, hatred, liver and stomach problems	Completion of physical health
Physical power, emotions and sexuality	Physical and sexual health, strength, vigor	Loss of appetite or libido, purposelessness, jealousy, infertility	Physical strengthening and growth
Life force, instinct, self-protection	Courage, self-esteem	Selfishness, anxiousness, rage, back problems, constipation	Physical birth

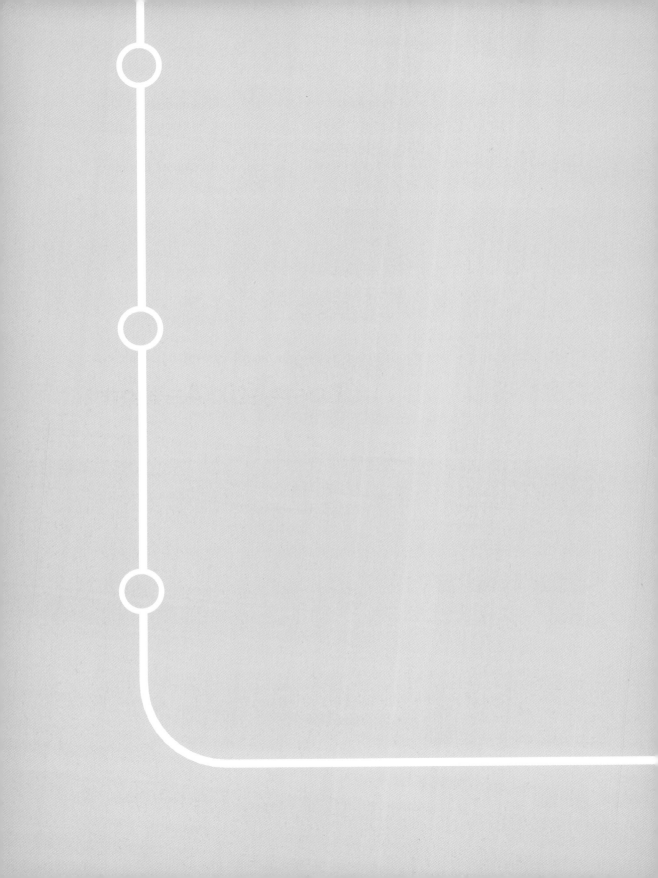

Part II
Energetic Anatomy

The Three Bodies

When you hear the word *body*, you probably think first and foremost of your physical body. But do you realize that you actually have three? Really, you use the other two bodies all the time, but they are not tangible, so it is easy to underestimate their importance.

One of these two nonphysical bodies is called the energy body. This energy body surrounds and extends beyond your physical body, interacting with the environment and with other people's energy bodies. Some people can even see this energy, which is called an *aura*. The seven chakras have a direct relationship with the energy body. If one chakra is particularly activated, then the associated color will dominate the aura.

Even if you cannot see this energy field, you can probably sense it. People's energy body is often directly reflective of the person's mental and spiritual state. For example, if someone walks in the room angry, you can probably sense it, even if they provide no visual clues. You can sense this because your energy body is affected by those of people around you. As you progress through this book's exercises, you will learn to sense and control your energy body more accurately.

An imbalance in the energy body often originates from spiritual problems. You can affect the state of the energy body with your thoughts and state of mind. If your mind receives negative information, or generates negative emotions, it will influence your energy body accordingly. We often think that physical diseases have only physical causes; however, before a disease or illness is physically manifested, it can be predicted by a pattern of energy imbalance.

Finally, we have a spiritual body, which surrounds both the physical and energy bodies and is the master of both. It, too, is an energy body of sorts, but it represents the divine aspect of the human being, connecting us to the heavenly dimension. All three

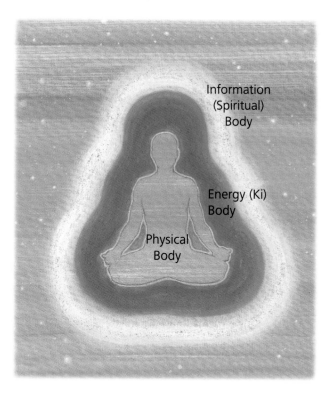

bodies form an organic relationship, influencing each other and determining our physical, mental, and emotional health.

The energy body acts as a bridge connecting our physical and spiritual bodies. In order for us to influence transformation of the body and mind, we must first learn to transform the energy flow. The ultimate purpose of Healing Chakras is the use of energy to effect the completion of the soul. In a sense, energy is the language with which you can communicate with your soul. Without knowing energy, it is not easy to approach your soul.

Chakras and the Body and Brain

The chakras are reflective of the individual's consciousness. In other words, your chakras are activated according to that which you focus on the most. Many people spend most of their time activating the first, second, and third chakras. Since the brain is the seat of consciousness, it follows that our chakra system is also affected by the brain.

Sexual appetite, fear, anxiety, desire, and despair are manifested when consciousness is trapped at the level of the lower three chakras. Unfortunately, we currently live in a society obsessed with sex, money, and other physical and material desires. This mind-set leaves individuals in an imbalanced state of being, while also contributing to an unhealthy cultural and natural environment.

Chakras also have a direct symbiotic relationship with the autonomic nervous system, the system that controls basic life functions, like respiration, circulation, and digestion. In addition, the chakras have an intimate relationship with the endocrine system. Blockages or imbalances in the energy of the chakras are reflected in the types and levels of hormones released by the endocrine system.

Conversely, pain or problems in a particular area of the physical body are transmitted to the corresponding chakra. For example, the sexual organs are connected to the first chakra, the digestive organs are connected to the second chakra, and so forth.

Full activation of the chakra system is an important matter not only for the individual, but for all of human society as well. When we activate the fourth through the seventh chakras, and utilize their connection to the profound energies of the universe, we will stimulate and awaken higher planes of human existence, consisting of wisdom, love, mercy, and insight, among others.

Activating the Chakras as They Relate to the Brain

Chakras may be activated one by one or as a whole system. Each chakra, once activated, will stimulate the associated area of the brain. For example, activating the fourth chakra, the heart chakra, will stimulate the brain to generate emotions. Activating the third chakra will generate a strong sense of the self.

The human brain is a very complex organ. At any given moment, different parts of your brain are being activated as millions of bioelectric impulses are flashing from one neuron to the next. Different parts of the brain communicate in a continual chorus of neuronal chatter. Neuroscientists are only beginning to understand the details of how our brains process thoughts and execute skills.

To simplify matters, however, it is helpful to view the brain in terms of three basic layers, each layer corresponding to a previous evolutionary stage: reptilian, mammalian, and human.

The reptilian brain is simple, geared only to basic survival functions: respiration, digestion, circulation, and reproduction. These functions are largely controlled subconsciously by the brain stem.

[The three layers of the human brain]

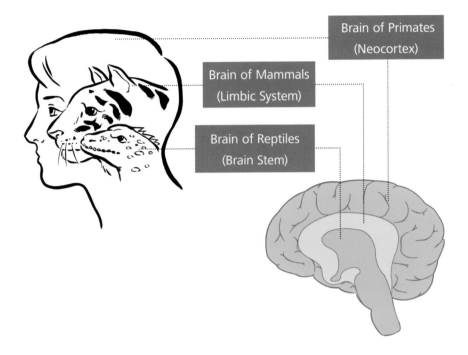

Brain of Primates
(Neocortex)

Brain of Mammals
(Limbic System)

Brain of Reptiles
(Brain Stem)

The mammalian brain adds the capacity for emotion and complex coordination of movement, which is associated with the limbic systems. The third phase of evolution resulted in the cerebral cortex, which provides the ability to solve problems, to be creative, and to analyze information.

The success of the human species is largely dependant upon our highly developed cerebral cortex, thus we can refer to this as the "human brain."

Reptilian Brain – 1st and 2nd Chakras

The brain stem consists of various sub-cortical structures. It maintains basic survival functions, including respiration, digestion, circulation, and reproduction. It corresponds to human's deepest subconscious, often becoming the major driving force behind life. Most people spend their time satisfying the needs of the first and second chakras, which includes satisfying the need for food, shelter, and sexual release.

Mammalian Brain – 3rd and 4th Chakras

Corresponds to the limbic system of the brain, the evolutionary second layer. Controls emotions such as joy, sadness, excitement, surprise, amazement, and love, among others. A problem with the limbic layer will create abnormal emotional responses. The limbic system also controls anger, fear, guilt, worry, pain, joy, and a range of other human emotional responses.

Human Brain – 5th and 6th Chakras

Corresponds to the neocortex, which enables us to create and introspect. Of these, the frontal lobe is the latest creation, giving us the ability to think and speculate. The ability of the neocortex to have insight, think, and rationalize helps to activate the fifth and sixth chakras. Therefore, a frontal lobotomy will often result in lack of imagination and interest in life. The neocortex is the mastermind behind all the glory of the human culture and civilization that we have created.

Light, Sound, and Vibration

Chakras are awakened and activated through energy. Energy exists in three forms: light, sound, and vibration.

Vibration is the quickest way to approach and stimulate the brain stem, which controls all basic life functions. Chakra activation begins with stimulation of the brain stem. Vibration is the essence of all of life's activities. All life, including each cell of our bodies, has a frequency of vibration. From the tiniest grain of sand to the largest of stars, all matter has a unique, characteristic frequency of vibration. It is the grand vibration of the cosmos that forms the essence of the grand harmony of the universe, within which chaos, creation, and evolution are generated.

Light, sound, and vibration exist within our bodies. Each of our internal organs has its characteristic and unique sound. Just as the heart beats, the brain, liver, stomach, kidneys, and other organs have their respective voices, which combined form a beautiful symphony.

Through vibration, our bodies continuously shed old cells and create new ones. This is a normal life process. By utilizing the natural healing power within all of us, persons with a healthy vibration can heal themselves, even when confronted with injury or illness. If a particular organ has a problem, it begins to emit a discordant tone. The rest of the body's organs then generate a harmonious, healing symphony, in an attempt to resolve the problem by helping the compromised organ regain its proper frequency. However, once the body's harmonious voice is weakened or broken, its healing power is compromised. Thus, illness can manifest. Negative thoughts are the primary cause of the breakdown, leading to discordant notes among the body's organs.

Healing Chakras training is designed to help each person recognize the naturally occurring rhythm of vibration within themselves. And further, to discover that it is a part of the overall symphony of the universe.

Part III

Chakras and Your Spiritual Development

The Secret Tradition
of Chakra Healing

Flowing within our bodies is the energy that drives and maintains our life functions. This energy flows not only within our bodies, but also through the very fabric of the universe. In Asian traditions, people call this energy *ki*, *chi*, or *prana*. There are seven major points of intersection for the flow of this energy in our bodies. These points are called chakras, or in the Korean tradition, *dahn-jons*.

Chakra, a Sanskrit word, means a wheel or a circle. This is appropriate because energy tends to swirl in a circular motion as it gathers in the chakras. In the ancient Asian mind-body-spirit discipline of Shin-sun-do (Way of the Divine), chakras are called *dahn-jons*. Literally translated, *dahn-jon* means "field where energy gathers."

Knowledge of the chakras has long been important in the Vedas and yoga of India, as well as other Asian traditions. Due to the importance of this knowledge to spiritual traditions of the East, and to the exclusivity of transmission of this information, the chakras may have been a bit overly mythologized. They have been relegated to the realm of the fantastic and have become inaccessible to the average person.

Even in the Korean Shin-sun-do tradition, only a very few, select individuals were lucky enough to find a teacher to guide them. In this tradition, "Small Universe" is the state in which all of the chakras are activated, all meridians of the body flow freely, and the mind and body become one. "Great Universe" is the state in which cosmic and bodily energy merge into one continuous and conscious flow, allowing discovery of the True Self.

A similar philosophy is expressed in Kundalini yoga. This tradition was similarly limited to a very select group of individuals. Kundalini means "life energy coiled in the shape of a snake

A picture from *Sung-myung-ji-gwe,* a 16TH Century book on the practice of Shin-sun-do. The pathways of the "Great Universe"—various Dahn-jons or chakras—are symbolized by drawings of a pot, crescent moon, and stars, among others.

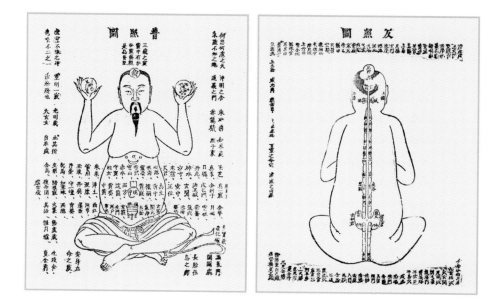

at the bottom of the spine." It is said that when the coiled life energy awakens, the energy will travel up the spine through the chakras and effect a spiritual awakening.

Chakras have an intimate relationsip with the spiritual growth of a person. To experience and understand the chakras means that you understand the flow of life, including the meaning of life and death. You might possess the most precious of gems, yet, if you don't know its value, then there is no difference between the gem and an ordinary pebble. One of the primary reasons that people are in constant search for "meaning" in life is that they don't understand the chakra system within their own bodies. Understanding the True Self, and thereby life's meaning and purpose, lies in an understanding of the chakras. Experiencing the chakras will bring about an overall understanding of life.

In the ancient Asian mind-body-spirit discipline of Shin-sun-do (Way of the Divine), there is a system for achieving spiritual completion through the chakras. Healing chakras training is a modernized version of this ancient system of advancing the spiritual journey, adapted for modern times.

It is with the hope of utilizing this system of Shin-sun-do to effectively awaken the potential of the seven chakras, that I write this book. The name "Healing Chakras" is simply the term I use for this modernized version of traditional Asian chakra training.

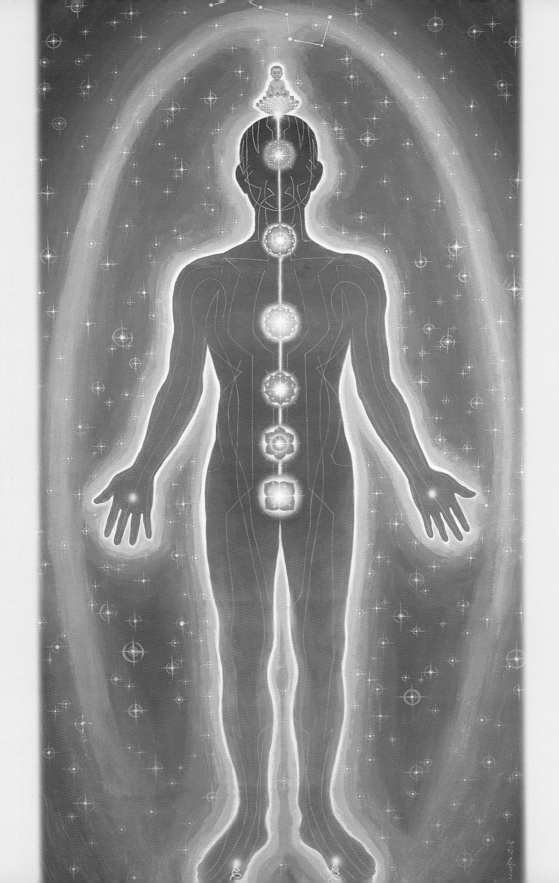

Secrets of
Heavenly Transformation
of Shin-sun-do

In the ancient tradition of Korea, there existed a body-mind-spirit training system that sought to elevate human consciousness to its highest plateau, that of divinity. Known by the name Shin-sun-do, meaning "Way of the Divine," the philosophy and ideas contained therein were originally derived from an ancient sacred text called *Chun-Bu-Kyung*, or *The Heavenly Code.*

This ancient Korean spiritual text is said to have been recorded by an ancient sage who realized his own enlightenment through his Shin-Sun-Do training regimen, through which he gaining insight into the realities of life and death and the operational flow of the universe. Because the *Chun-Bu-Kyung* is essentially a numerical representation of the laws of the cosmos, it cannot be interpreted literally. It will only fully reveal its true nature and meaning to someone who has experienced the realities of life through the study of ki energy.

One of the key concepts of the *Chun-Bu-Kyung* is the triad of heaven, Earth, and human. Through this concept, you can glimpse the ultimate meaning and purpose of human existence. The text places the human being as the intermediary between heaven and Earth, suggesting that mankind's highest purpose is to bridge the earthly and heavenly realms. Although we are born into a physical body with many attributes similar to those of other living creatures on the planet, according to this philosophy we have a special mission to develop our divine aspect and to reconnect to the heavenly sphere.

Years ago, I completed a severe twenty-one-day training program similar to those used in the Sun-do cultures of long ago. At the end of this training, I experienced a profound sense of oneness with the universe, something commonly referred to as "enlightenment." At that time, I did not know that the nature of my enlightenment was already spoken of in the *Chun-Bu-Kyung*. When I finally had the good fortune to learn of it, I realized that my enlightenment encapsulated within the *Chun-Bu-Kyung*.

Upon reading the *Chun-Bu-Kyung*, I could sense the energy in each one of its eighty-one letters when I sank deeply into meditation. The teachings of the *Chun-Bu-Kyung* came to me not through the intellect, but through actual experience of its energies. When I experienced the oneness of heaven, Earth, and human as described in the *Chun-Bu-Kyung*, I felt the intense joy of becoming part of the light of the cosmos.

When we realize our innate divine potential, we become one with the essence of the universe. We become one with creativity, peace, and love. Currently in our world, we are trapped in the illusion that we must be in constant competition with one another. We live with the belief that you and I are different and separate. The *Chun-Bu-Kyung* contains the essence of the trinity, in which good and evil, life and death, heaven and Earth are not defined as opposites, but as parts of the same cosmic harmony. When we realize that our essence is identical to the essence that makes up the cosmos, we overcome fear, sadness, and anger.

Oneness, where no barrier exists between you and me, is our essence and our divinity. As soon as we are born, we begin the struggle to light up this innate divinity. Once we realize our own divine enlightenment, we reach the highest level of awareness, and consciously return to the Source at the moment of death. This is the process that is delineated in the letters of the *Chun-Bu-Kyung.*

Living for the Growth of the Soul

The spiritual goal of Healing Chakras training is to acknowledge the soul, become consciously aware of its living presence, and act to nurture its growth. The answers to such questions as: "Why was I born?" and "What is my life's purpose?" and "What do I live for?" are already within you. Yet, without knowing our soul, we are prisoners of our physical bodies. Since the body is a creature of space and time, it begins its march toward death as soon as it is born. When the body dies off, as it inevitably will, what is left? The soul.

Every human being has "divinity" that is of the same essence as the source of the cosmos. Our bodies act as temporary housing for the journey of our souls. We came to the Earth in order to go forward and complete the journey of our soul. Although our physical bodies have their limitations, they also contain the necessary tools to propel our souls toward completion of the journey. The difficulties and trials that come with the human body are actually blessings, propelling our souls' expansive growth.

The chakras are vitally important to the growth of the soul because it is through energy that we can reconnect to our divine nature. While the heavenly and Earthly spheres may seem vastly different, energy is the common factor that unites both elements. Energy is like the language spoken in both realms. Thus, learning to understand our life energy helps us meet with and complete our souls.

We are not merely physical beings. Our soul, the essence of our nature, transcends time and space. Everyone has this eternal life within them. Only when the eyes of your soul open can you recognize the existence of the divinity within you. When you realize that you are the essence of eternal life, you will be free from fear, loneliness, and grief.

Healing Chakras is a training to recognize your True Self, your true essence. Is my body my True Self? Is my soul my True Self? My True Self is my divinity, my soul, and my energy. When you realize that you are eternal, you will realize that life and death are just expressions of the essence of life in different forms. Just as the moon remains essentially the same while its visible shape changes according to where the shadows fall, the essence of life remains the same while its visible shape changes. The sun is beautiful when it rises. It is also beautiful when it sets. Although we cannot see the sun at night, it has not ceased to exist. Our life may seem all too brief when seen from a limited point of view, but actually it is eternal. This is because the underlying reality of life does not change.

For the person who is grounded in the timeless truth of the universe, there is no life and no death. He or she can experience eternal joy without being limited by the definitions of good and evil. The essence of Oneness always exists within us.

Chakras and the Heavenly Code

Within the letters of the *Chun-Bu-Kyung* lie the principles and purpose of Healing Chakras. The Heavenly Code can be interpreted as an expression of mathematics, philosophy, and even energy studies. Each letter of the Heavenly Code contains its own distinct letter or numerical meaning when read, and distinct energy or musical characteristics when sounded. It combines number/ratio and sound/energy characteristics of the individual components into a holistic effect, which is an actual representation of the principle of harmonious order. When the effects of the Heavenly Code are applied to the human chakra system, we can begin to understand the underlying principles of Healing Chakras.

The *Chun-Bu-Kyung* also provides humanity with a clear sense of meaning and purpose in life. A key concept in the text is the triad of heaven, Earth, and human. According to the scripture, mankind exists as a bridge between heaven and Earth; this truth is also contained within the human chakra system, which contains energies ranging from the animal (lower chakras) to the divine (upper chakras). As we open our chakra system, we complete this bridge between heaven and Earth.

The Heavenly Code describes life as a journey for completion of the soul, a way of heavenly transformation. This journey of the soul's completion coincides with the activation of the seven chakras. From the point of view of the "Way of Heavenly Transformation," the seven chakras consist of three gates and three palaces, giving rise to the third birth in a human life.

天符經
Chun-Bu-Kyung

一 始 無 始 一 析 三 極 無
Il Shi Mu Shi Il Sok Sam Guk Mu

盡 本 天 一 一 地 一 二 人
Jin Bon Chun Il Il Ji Il Ee In

一 三 一 積 十 鉅 無　化 Il
Il Sam Il Juk Ship Guh Mu Gwe Hwa

三 天 二 三 地 二 三 人 二
Sam Chun Ee Sam Ji Ee Sam In Ee

三 大 三 合 六 生 七 八 九
Sam Dae Sam Hap Yuk Saeng Chil Pal Goo

運 三 四 成 環 五 七 一 妙
Woon Sam Sah Sung Hwan Oh Chil Il Myo

衍 萬 往 萬 來 用 變 不 動
Yeon Man Wang Man Rae Yong Byun Bu Dong

本 本 心 本 太 陽 昂 明 人
Bon Bon Shim Bon Tae Yang Ang Myung In

中 天 地 一 一 終 無 終 一
Joong Chun Ji Il Il Jong Mu Jong Il

One begins unmoved moving that has no beginning.
One divides to three crowns
While remaining a limitless mover.
Heaven comes first,
Earth comes second,
Human comes third.
One gathers to build ten,
And infinite forms become the trinity
of heaven, Earth, human.
Heaven gains two to make three,
Earth gains two to make three,
Human gains two to make three.
Three trinities make six,
And they create seven and eight. Nine appears,
And there comes a turning.
Three and four form a circle;
Five with seven makes one whole.
Wayless is the way. All comes and all goes.
Features are changing, and changeless is the Maker.
Divine mind is eternal light,
Looking toward celestial light.
Human bears heaven and Earth,
And the three make One.
One is the end of all,
And the One has no ending.

The Principle of Creation and Evolution

一始無始 (Il Shi Mu Shi)
One begins unmoved moving that has no beginning.

一析三極無盡本 (Il Sok Sam Guk Mu Jin Bon)
One divides to three crowns while remaining a limitless mover.

天一一地一二人一三 (Chun Il Il Ji Il Ee In Il Sam)
Heaven comes first; Earth comes second; human comes third.

一積十鉅無化三 (Il Juk Ship Guh Mu Gwe Hwa Sam)
One gathers to build ten, and infinite forms become the trinity.

天二三地二三人二三 (Chun Ee Sam Ji Ee Sam In Ee Sam)
Heaven gains two to make three, Earth gains two to make three,
Human gains two to make three.

大三合六生七八九運
(Dae Sam Hap Yook Saeng Chil Pal Gu Woon)
Three trinities make six, and they create seven and eight.
Nine appears, and there comes a turning.

In numbers one through nine, the number six becomes a transition point. After going through six, life goes on to seven, eight, and nine, before going back to one. Everything, in its naturally ordained time, goes through deep renewal, a cosmic hibernation. Likewise, death is not really death. Once freed from the confines of the physical body, the soul evolves and assumes form in a higher dimension. Just as everything began with the One and will ultimately return to the One, the soul can be said to have completed its journey once it returns to where it came from.

The number six is also crucial in the human chakra system. It refers not only to the sixth chakra of our body, but also to the Birth of the Soul" from the place of the sixth chakra." In the Heavenly Code six is related to "be born or revive life." If the first chakra is the gate through which the body is born, then the sixth chakra is the gate through which the soul is born. Once you have awakened to the birth of your soul, you are no longer fettered to the body, but can develop the "sight" to see life as an eternal force that exists in itself, of itself, and by itself.

The Principle of Water Up, Fire Down

三四成環五七一 (Sam Sah Sung Hwan Oh Chil Il)
Three and four form a circle; five with seven makes one whole.

妙衍萬汪萬來用變不動本
(Myo Yeon Man Wang Man Rae Yong Byun Bu Dong Bon)
Wayless is the way. All comes and all goes.
Features are changing, and changeless is the Maker.

Water Energy Up, Fire Energy Down (Su-Seung-Hwa-Gang) refers to the direction in which energy must flow in the body in order to create harmony and a healthy balance. Water energy must travel up the energy channels along the spine, while fire energy must travel down the energy channels along the center-line of the front of the body. This condition indicates the optimal state of energy flow.

82

The word *three* in the first line above refers to the three main internal chakras, the second, the fourth, and the sixth. The word *four* in the first line above refers to the four external chakras, located on each of the palms and the bottoms of both feet. The external chakras located in the center of each palm are called *Jang-shim*, and the external chakras located in the center of each foot are called *Yong-chun*. When the three major internal chakras and the four external chakras are working as one circle, the body is filled with free-flowing life energy in accordance with the direction of Water Energy Up, Fire Energy Down.

The "five with seven makes one wholw" in the line above refers to the fifth, seventh, and first chakras. When these chakras, which are the three gates of life, are connected with the other four internal chakras (second, third, fourth, sixth), and with the four major external chakras, the life force within us will flow freely, bringing infinite creativity and joy to the soul.

本心本太陽昂明 (Bon Shim Bon Tae Yang Ang Myung)
Divine mind is eternal light, looking toward celestial light.

This phrase means that when the mind is at its proper center, then the mind becomes as bright as the sun. Mind is placed in the fourth chakra. When the fourth chakra is awakened and becomes bright, it shall awaken the first, fifth, and seventh chakras, thereby attaining freedom of the soul. Someone who has attained true freedom of the soul is called "Shin In," or Divine Person. When the soul attains true freedom, it escapes the limitations of the body, without life or death, beginning or end, and reaches the place of the One. Healing Chakras training is, therefore, based on the principle of activating the chakra system for the purpose of enlightening divinity within for completion of the soul's journey.

The Principle of the Oneness of the Cosmic Self

人中天地一 (In Joong Chun Ji Il)
Human bears heaven and Earth, and the three make One.

"Human Bears Heaven and Earth" refers to the person who has realized the Self as part of the Grand Oneness of the cosmos. Such a person is also a "Shin In," or divine person. Healing Chakras is a training system designed to allow one to experience the Self as part of the whole cosmos. When all seven internal chakras are awakened, or activated, you will realize Oneness with the rest of the cosmos, knowing that heaven and Earth are within you.

The Principle of Eternal Life

一終無終一 (Il Jong Mu Jong Il)
One is the end of all, and the One has no ending.

The physical body has a beginning and an end. However, the soul is timeless and limitless. Knowing this, you are liberated from fear, attaining true peace of mind, freedom of imagination, and infinite creativity of the spirit. When the soul leaves a person's body through the seventh chakra, that individual is said to have undergone a Heavenly Transformation.

The Chakras and the Completion of the Soul

There are three gates and three palaces, which we must pass through in order to attain completion of the soul. Awakening the chakras, by ascending the chakra ladder, will lead you to the third human birth, the spiritual birth of Heavenly Transformation.

The Three Gates

Jade Gate (First Chakra):
Signifies the first chakra, located at the perineum. It is the gate through which the seed of life enters. It is also the gate through which the body is born. Life's first birth, the birth of the body, occurs through the Jade Gate.

Soul Gate (Fifth Chakra):
Signifies the fifth chakra, located around the thyroid glands in the neck. The soul is trapped in the physical body. In order for a soul to be

born through the sixth chakra, it must escape the fourth and pass through the fifth chakra. When the Soul Gate opens, the seed of the soul enters the palace of the sixth chakra to begin growing. Once you pass through the Soul Gate, you will feel a true sense of freedom. You will no longer be deceived by the cycle of highs and lows based on material gain and external circumstances. When you attain true freedom of the soul, frustration and emptiness will disappear naturally.

Heaven's Gate (Seventh Chakra):
Also called the Great Heaven's Gate, this refers to the seventh chakra, located at the crown of the head. Its literal meaning is "Gate that connects to Heaven." In Asia, this energy center was much revered. Just as the body gestates in the womb and is born through the Jade Gate, the soul gestates in the palace of the sixth chakra and is born through Heaven's Gate. This is the birth of the spiritual body.

The Three Palaces

Earth Palace (Second Chakra):
This is the place where sperm and ovum meet to create and nurture the body. It is often referred to as the Earth Palace because it is the place where the body is prepared for birth into life on Earth.

Mind Palace (Fourth Chakra):
This is referred to as the Mind Palace because it is believed to house the energy of the mind. It is also the place of emotions, including loneliness, sadness, and love. Someone who is full of compassion and love is often referred to as a "humane" person. In order to open Heaven's Gate, all of the chakras from the first through the seventh must be connected. The fourth chakra is especially important in this connection. You must open your mind and rid yourself of attachment and greed in order to awaken the fourth chakra.

Heaven's Palace (Sixth Chakra):
This is the place where the soul dwells with the presence of heaven. When the soul passes through the Soul's Gate (fifth chakra) and enters into Heaven's Palace, it begins to mature, readying itself for a spiritual birth through Heaven's Gate (seventh chakra).

The Three Births

Human beings have the potential to undergo three separate births. First is the physical birth, in which the body is born through the Jade Gate of the first chakra. Second is the awakening, in which you realize that the essence of your being is your soul. This awakening occurs in the sixth chakra. The third birth refers to the birth of the spiritual body through Heaven's Gate, the seventh chakra. When you have achieved the third birth, you will have attained oneness with the cosmos, completion of the soul.

The body is akin to a vehicle driven by the soul. The body must be left behind in order for the soul to be born through Heaven's Gate. The analogy is rather simple. In order for you to enter the house, you have to get out of your vehicle. You only need the car to get you to your house. In order for your soul to be born through Heaven's Gate, it must mature and become complete. The picture of a small baby on top of the head in the chakra drawing refers to this spiritual birth, a Heavenly Transformation.

In the tradition of Shin-Sun-Do, the process of the completion and birth of the soul is called "Sung Tong Gong Wan." "Sung Tong" refers to awakening, or enlightenment. "Gong Wan" refers to the real effort and work required for a person to actualize enlightenment in the real world. Therefore, the process involves both profound internal awakening and real effort to actualize this new awareness in the world.

Healing Chakras and the Soul

Do you remember your immediate past? I am not asking you to recall your previous lives, but rather to think about your recent past in this life on a biological level. This may be a trick question of sorts, but no less true because of it.

You were a sperm. And you were an ovum. Then, you were an embryo and a fetus. Then, you were a baby, born into this world with the body of a human being. Some of you were received warmly, while others of you were not. This is not too important in the overall scheme of things. Do you know the odds of being born as a human being, not in a metaphysical sense, but in a biological sense?

In the Buddhist tradition, they say the odds of being born as a human being are the same odds as a sea turtle encountering a wooden plank floating in the middle of the Pacific Ocean as it comes up for air. Let's examine the odds in a biological sense. We all know how a baby is conceived. With each ejaculation, between 100 and 150 million sperm are released. Of those, only one has a chance to fertilize the ovum, resulting in conception. So, the odds of conception are about 1 in 100 million. However, the odds are actually even higher than this, since not every sexual encounter will result in either ejaculation or the introduction of sperm into the vagina. Frankly, calculating all the social factors that go into a couple's decision to bear a child, the odds of a human being as unique as you being born is truly unimaginable. The odds are literally astronomical. Being born as a human being is akin to a roll of the cosmic dice. That is why birth as a human being is a great blessing, too great to truly articulate.

But, what is the purpose of being born as a human being? To attain the physical body? No. You already know that the purpose of a human birth is to complete the journey of your soul, to manifest your essence as a spiritual being, to effect the birth of your spiritual body. This is also the purpose of the chakra system and Healing Chakras.

So, how do we achieve this completion? We can explain the process of spiritual birth using the chakra system. We can think about this process of spiritual birth as part of our natural anatomy. To initiate the process of our physical birth, the sperm enters through the Jade Gate, the first chakra, and lodges in the Earth Palace or Womb, the second chakra. A life is conceived when the sperm joins with an ovum. After nine months of gestation, the physical body matures and is born, once again passing through the Jade Gate. These are the fundamentals of our reproductive system.

Now, let's think about the spiritual birth process. The sperm is analogous to the seed of the soul, while the ovum is analogous to the divinity within us. The spiritual sperm, or seed of the soul, is not some abstract concept, however. It resides in the heart, the fourth chakra, intertwined with the presence of energy there. Then where does the spiritual ovum reside? It lives in the sixth chakra, which is also called Heaven's Palace. Therefore, the process of spiritual birth is ignited when the spiritual sperm and the spiritual ovum merge in Heaven's Palace, the spiritual womb within the human body. In order for the merging to take effect, the spiritual sperm, like the physical sperm, must pass through a gate. This gate is the fifth chakra, or the Soul's Gate. When the seed of the soul passes through the Soul's Gate and lodges in Heaven's Palace, where it meets with inner divinity, a spiritual embryo is conceived. After a process of maturation and growth, the spiritual body is born through the seventh chakra, also called the Great Heaven's Gate.

Now you understand the meaning behind the terms that we use to denote the individual chakras. It is this process of spiritual birth that differentiates us from other animals. It is why human beings are spiritual beings. Therefore, as a human being, you have an incredible opportunity to express your spiritual essence in a profound way. Once your spiritual body is born, you are ready to merge with Cosmic Energy and Cosmic Mind, the essence of the Creator. You are a child of the Creator, holding the seed of the Creator Within. You are the sons and daughters of God.

The chakra system serves as the reservoir of the spiritual potential within us. If our physical body is our temple, then our energy body, as represented by the chakra system, is our altar upon which we will stand and rise to our rightful place as a spiritual being, in tune with the great truth and cycle of the cosmos. To achieve this is our ultimate goal in life. Healing Chakras is our way of beginning this journey of the soul.

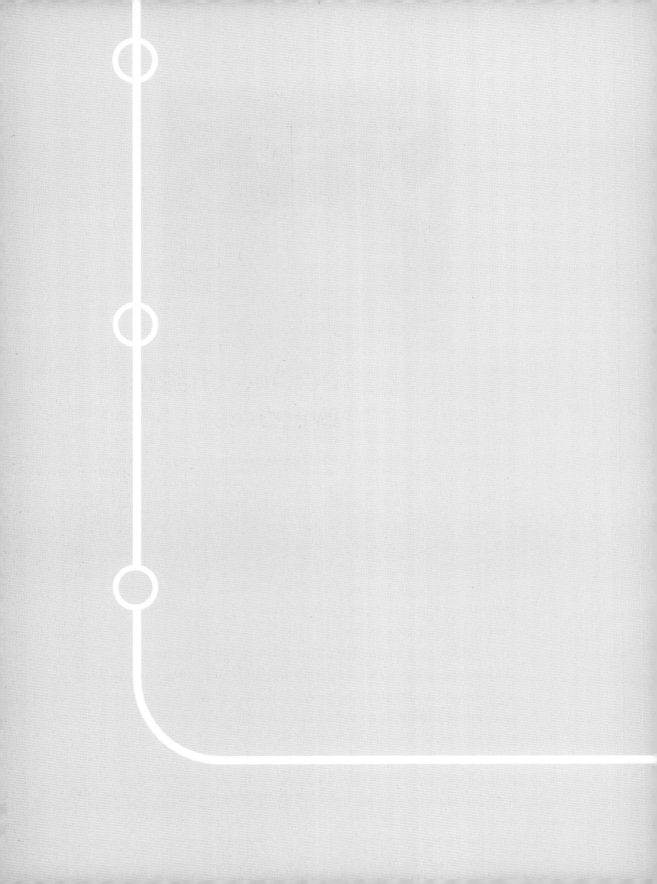

Part IV
Healing Chakras
Exercises

Chakra Relaxation

Before beginning Healing Chakra training, it is important to relax your body and mind. Unless you are sensitive to ki energy, you cannot activate your body's chakra system effectively. Ki energy is felt when body and mind are in a relaxed state. Relaxation is a prerequisite to all forms of meditation and healing. When we are tense, our minds and bodies tend to contract, thus prohibiting the free flow of energy.

Ki energy acts as a bridge connecting body and soul. The soul delivers its messages to the body through ki energy. You must relax in order to meet with your soul. Energy Sensitivity Training(Ji-gam) and Energy Dance (Dahn-mu) are the most effective methods to induce relaxation. Energy Sensitivity Training assists in stopping the flow of thoughts and emotions, making it possible to concentrate exclusively on the body. With this heightened sensitivity, it is possible to expand the feeling of the subtle currents of energy. As your awareness of energy becomes deeper, your body will move with the flow of energy in an unconscious, spontaneous expression of the energy flow.

When you practice Energy Sensitivity Training, the sensation of energy usually begins in the hands and then quickly moves through the whole body until the entire body is responding in dancelike movement called Energy Dance.

These graceful motions come from deep within a person's being as perfect, spontaneous movements of self-expression. One begin to experience a gentle, dynamic meditation from a subconscious state.

Through ki energy, you can communicate with any organ of your body. Ki energy is omnipresent, not only within our bodies, but throughout the universe. Ki goes where our mind directs it. If we consciously think about our heart and brain, ki will flow there. Energy Dance is a way of expressing currents of energy with your movements. The moment you are immersed in the ever-flowing currents of energy, beyond all the barriers of self-consciousness and thought, you begin to converse with your soul. This is the moment when the divinity within awakens. You start understanding the true meaning of these statements: "My body is not everything I am." "My emotions are not everything I am." "My thoughts are not everything I am."

And you ask real questions to yourself. "Then, what or who am I?" "Who is the real me?" Through ki energy you can closely meet with your True Self. Energy Dance is a signal that you are ready to meet the Creator Within. To feel the flow of ki energy, and to use it to awaken the deepest potential within, is truly a blessing and will bring about a transformation of your life.

Self-Observation

❶ Sit or stand in a comfortable position and close your eyes.

❷ Let us take this opportunity to meet with the body. In order to meet with your body closely, you must first separate your consciousness from your body. Whisper to yourself . . .

My body is not me, but mine.
My mouth is not me, but mine.
My head is not me, but mine.
My eyes are not me, but mine.
My legs are not me, but mine.
My arms are not me, but mine.
My chest is not me, but mine.
My thoughts are not me, but mine.
My emotions are not me, but mine.

❸ Whisper to yourself continuously, as you feel every part of your body, from your head to your toes . . . Whisper to yourself with confidence and conviction, until you feel yourself looking at your body.

❹ Normally, we are not aware of our sensory organs. We rarely think of our senses as separate from ourselves. This is why we are tricked into thinking that the phenomena we perceive through our senses are the substances of reality. Try to feel your "sensory self." Your "self," with eyes, nose, ears, thoughts, and emotions, is looking at your body comfortably and peacefully.

Energy Sensitivity Training

❶ Raise both hands to chest level, palms facing each other, but not touching.

❷ Direct your consciousness to your hands and whisper, "Hands . . . hands . . . hands . . ." with the voice of your mind.

❸ Feel your hands begin to react, feeling a certain pull, warmth . . . something drifting between your hands. You are feeling the sensation of energy.

❹ Now push your hands closer together. When you think, "My hands are coming closer together . . . " Then they will draw closer. When you think, "My hands are moving farther apart." Then they will move away from each other. You can control your hands with your mind. Repeat the pull–push motions, affirming the sensation of energy between your hands.

❺ Now, imagine a ball of energy between your hands. Pour your consciousness into the space between your hands.

Feel the cloud of energy, tangible and alive. Expand the living sensation, molding it into the shape of a ball. Smooth the edges until it becomes a sphere . . . a ball full of air and energy.

❻ You have just created a ball of energy with your hands. Such is the way of energy and your mind. This is the source that will free the energies of your chakras.

❼ When you concentrate on a certain part of your body, blood flows to that part, energy gathers, and heat generates. A pulse beats and a magnetic energy exists. Consciousness communicates with the brain. The brain sends blood where you will it to go, and energy follows.

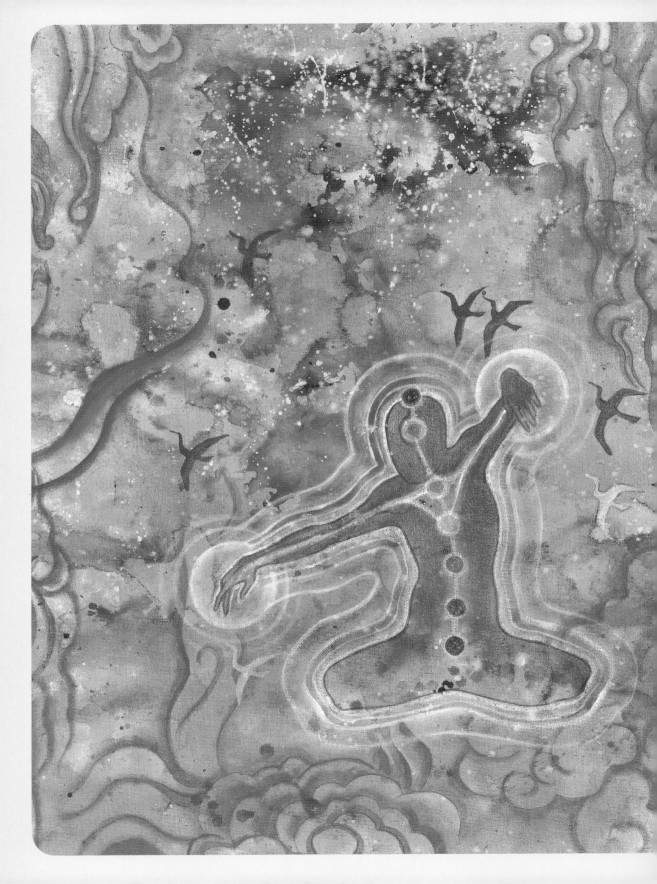

Energy Dance

❶ Repeat the Energy Sensitivity Training and gradually increase the feeling of energy.

❷ While immersing yourself into the feeling of energy through the motions of opening and closing the hands, let your whole body move naturally with the flow of energy.

❸ Let the currents of energy take you where they will. Let go of logic and rational thought. Let exuberance and spontaneity take over. You no longer feel any weight in your hands. They are floating freely in the gentle current of the great sea of energy. Your hands, your neck, your shoulders . . . all are moving freely. Your arms, legs, and waist . . . all dance without gravity.

❹ Your left-brain might rule your day. Logical, rational, and strict . . . a prison of limited information and memory. Now, rest your left brain and give your right brain free rein. For your right brain knows what you need. Let the right brain move you in all the right ways . . . in all the right places . . . to fill you with passion, love, and peace . . . and clear your tangled thoughts and emotions. Feel the chakras move and stir as your soul calls out for freedom.

❺ Hold a conversation with your soul as you do the Energy Dance. It will move you with the flow of energy. It is unlike any way you have ever moved, unlike any dance you have ever danced. Thoughts move your body through nerves as the soul moves your body through energy. You are experiencing your soul. You are relaxed and purified.

Feeling Your Chakras

Locating the Chakras in Your Body

At first, due to unfamiliarity, it is difficult to feel the exact location of the chakras within your body. The first step in the process is to identify the location of each chakra and to focus on the feeling until you become familiar with its sensation. After a while, with concentration, you will quickly be able to locate the sensation of the individual chakras.

As seen in the diagram, the chakras are located roughly along the line of your spine. Because chakras are energy centers, they do not necessarily correspond to specific anatomical locations. Since the chakras are energy centers, they are not visible, like blood and bones. Therefore, it is easier to try to imagine the exact location of each chakra by locating its corresponding point on the front of the body. By identifying general physical landmarks on the front of the body, it will be possible to communicate the location of specific chakras on which to concentrate.

From the first through the seventh chakra, we will touch upon the sensation of each individual chakra.

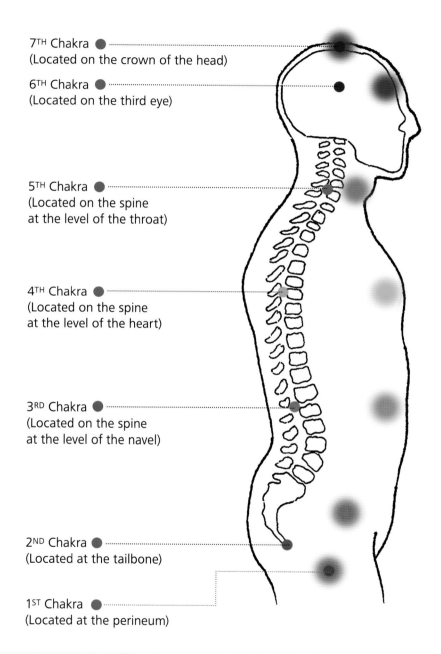

7TH Chakra
(Located on the crown of the head)

6TH Chakra
(Located on the third eye)

5TH Chakra
(Located on the spine
at the level of the throat)

4TH Chakra
(Located on the spine
at the level of the heart)

3RD Chakra
(Located on the spine
at the level of the navel)

2ND Chakra
(Located at the tailbone)

1ST Chakra
(Located at the perineum)

Locations of the chakras, along the line of your spine, and their corresponding energy points along the front surface of the body. These energy points and physical landmarks will help in feeling and visualizing each chakra.

First Chakra - Hwe-um

❶ Sit in half lotus position with your back straight.

❷ Concentrate on the first chakra. Men should concentrate on your perineum, between the anus and base of the penis. Women should concentrate on the back of the vagina between the urethra and anus. If you can't feel the area, contract and relax your sphincter muscle repeatedly.

❸ As you repeat this exercise, imagine a stream of energy coming in and out of the first chakra. Men should concentrate on the feeling of pressure on the perineum. Women should concentrate on the feeling near the opening of the vagina. Through repeated contraction/relaxation of the sphincter muscle you can awaken the sensation of the first chakra, amplifying the energy in the area. Repeat the contraction/relaxation of the sphincter muscle 100 times. You will have a sensation of heat, as energy courses through your body. A healthy first chakra is the color of clear red, imparting a feeling of warmth. A problematic first chakra turns to the color of a dying ember.

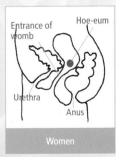

Women

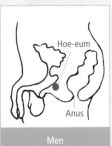

Men

106

Source of All Energy

A four-leaf lotus flower with a deep red color represents the first chakra. This chakra is the place where the body meets the Earth. It is the place where energy flows into the body. When this chakra is weak, energy can also be lost through this area. The first chakra is the source of all creation and growth, undulating with the pure energy of life. The first chakra must be fully functional in order to activate the other chakras. It acts as a pump that helps the stream of energy rise along the spine. This imparts a sense of confidence and a love of life, creating a positive energy field that influences others.

A person with a healthy first chakra is full of life and the will to grow. If your first chakra is blocked or impeded, you will experience a lack of will, vigor, and passion. Without sufficient physical energy, the body cannot act as a solid anchor for consciousness, resulting in the lack of a sense of reality. This may result in the appearance of illness and oversensitivity to external circumstances. Spiritual richness can only arise with plenty of energy.

Second Chakra - Dahn-jon

The second chakra is located at the very end of the tailbone. In order to activate the second chakra, concentrate on your lower abdomen (Dahn-jon), which is located about two inches below your navel. The second chakra connects to the prostate gland in men. In women, it is connected to the uterus. It is also connected to the reproductive organs, bladder, and kidneys.

❶ When you breathe in, imagine a stream of air entering your body through your lower back, the myung-mun point on the back side of the second chakra. Feel the energy curling and swirling as it enters . . . When you breathe out, imagine the stream of air uncurling as it exits.

❷ When you breathe in, your lower abdomen expands. When you breathe out, your lower abdomen contracts. Continue breathing as you are feeling your second chakra. You may feel emptiness in your second chakra. You may experience a feeling of fullness. Silently follow the path of your breath. You will feel warmth in your lower abdomen. You may feel a beating pulse coming alive. These are the sensations of your second chakra.

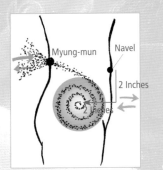

Creative and Sexual Energy

The symbol of the second chakra is a six-leaf, scarlet lotus flower. Along with the first chakra, the second chakra controls sexual energy. A person with a healthy second chakra has strength, while a person with a blocked second chakra easily feels fatigued.

The second chakra is where the Earth's energy, flowing in through the feet, combines with both the energy of heaven, coming in as you breathe, and the energy of life that exists within us all. Here these energies merge and are transformed into a higher form of energy. Energies gathered in the lower abdomen also stimulate the kidneys to elevate water energy and lower fire energy, facilitating optimal flow of energy according to the Water Up, Fire Down principle. This results in a relaxed mind, clear head, and strong physical power.

The second chakra mounts a defense system around the body to protect it from toxins in foodstuff, nervous disorders, and contagious diseases. It cleanses the body of deeply rooted tension and stress that inhibit procreative activities.

Activation of the second chakra also translates into maternal love and charity for others, resulting in harmonious relationships characterized by forgiveness and comfort. However, a blocked or impaired second chakra may lead to negativity and jealousy, which results in miscommunication with others. Dysfunction in this chakra may also lead to overbearing parental love based on control and domination.

Third Chakra - Joong-wahn

❶ The third chakra is located straight behind the navel. Concentrate on the spot two inches above your navel. Using your fingers, press on the point two inches above your navel.

❷ Now release the pressure of your fingers. Concentrate on the point just behind them. Feel the beating of your pulse. When you inhale, breath comes in through the third chakra. When you exhale, the breath goes out the same way.

❸ Observe the organs surrounding the third chakra with your mind's eye. The third chakra connects with the stomach. It also controls the liver, gallbladder, and pancreas.

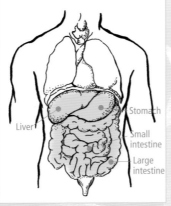

Liver

Stomach

Small intestine

Large intestine

110

Physical Digestion and Metabolism

A ten-leaf, orange lotus flower symbolizes the third chakra. A healthy third chakra is bright orange, while a weak or blocked one may be a whitish or even bluish color. The third chakra controls the body's metabolism and overall functioning. An active and healthy third chakra generates enthusiasm and passion for work. When the third chakra is operating properly and harmoniously, rich emotions are present. A weakened third chakra allows increased emotional vulnerability.

The third chakra relates to the element of fire and is located on the spot called the "solar plexus." It controls ambition and appetite, facilitating balanced metabolism. You can easily tell the state of your third chakra by observing your appetite. When the third chakra is weak, you will have a decreased appetite for food. Excessive appetite is also indicative of a chakra that is unbalanced.

The third chakra also connects with the neocortex. Accordingly, it is very sensitive to stress. If stress is prolonged, deterioration of the internal organs will occur. It is important to maintain a calm and peaceful state of mind in order to maximize efficiency of the third chakra and the internal organs. It also controls the liver, gallbladder, and pancreas.

Fourth Chakra - Dahn-joong

❶ The fourth chakra is located behind the heart, toward the back and middle of the chest. When you concentrate, concentrate on the slight indentation on your chest, or sternum.

❷ Using your fingers, press on your sternum. Now release the pressure of your fingers. Concentrate on the point just behind the pressure. Breathe in slowly and let your chest expand. Breathe out and let your chest contract. Breathe in . . . and breathe out. Imagine the breath streaming in and out of your fourth chakra.

❸ Concentrate on the fourth chakra, and expand the sensation. You are feeling the source of energy for love and devotion. Gently probe the state of your heart. Do you feel blocked or open, comfortable or stuffy? When the fourth chakra is weak, a major energy channel running through the chest may easily become blocked.

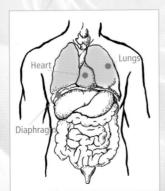

Our Humanness

A twelve-leaf golden lotus flower symbolizes the fourth chakra. The fourth chakra expands our energy and sends it in all directions in equal parts. It also acts to harmonize opposing energies, such as male/female, yin/yang, and emotional/logical. The fourth chakra is located right in the center of the chakra ladder. There are three chakras above it, and three below. When the fourth chakra, which links the energies of body and mind together, becomes active, you experience a sense of pure love and compassion. This arises out of a balance of mind and body.

The fourth chakra relates to the human attributes of love, forgiveness, honesty, responsibility, and diligence. A healthy fourth chakra creates a balanced and harmonious energy of love. It facilitates the balance of logic with emotion, and the real with the ideal, helping you to develop the maturity to be objective and unconditional in your love of others. You will give and receive love from a centered and balanced place.

Fifth Chakra - Chun-dol

❶ The fifth chakra is located just behind your throat, by the thyroid glands. Lightly press down on your throat, on the spot where a man's Adam's apple is located.

❷ Now, release the pressure of your fingers. Concentrate on the point just behind where the pressure was.

❸ Lightly touch the roof of your mouth with your tongue. Breathe in, as you imagine a stream of breath enter the fifth chakra. Breathe out as you imagine a stream of breath leaving through the same spot.

❹ Breathe in as you bend your head backward. Breathe out as you come back up. Breathe in as you bend your head forward. Breathe out as you come back up. Rotate your head from side to side.

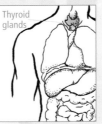

Thyroid glands

114

Energy of Purification and Harmony

A sixteen-leaf lotus flower is the symbol of the fifth chakra. It is a blue-green color with a tinge of yellow. The fifth chakra is the center for purification and cleansing. This chakra represents an open heart and mind. An open mind leads to a greater understanding of life. A person with an open mind goes through life embracing discomfort along with comfort, the bad along with the good . . . the vinegar with the wine. Such a person possesses the wisdom to go along with the flow of life.

A problem with the fifth chakra translates into a lack of emotional control and rapid fatigue arising out of hypersensitivity to change. This chakra is the bridge between aspects of the physical human and the spiritual human. It determines whether you live a more materialistic or a more spiritual life.

This is why we refer to the fifth chakra as the Soul's Gate. Without going through this gate, you cannot completely move into the realm of the spiritually divine. With the fifth chakra closed, emptiness of spirit drives an attempt to attain lasting fulfillment with riches and recognition. This emptiness is a message from your soul. We can experience true peace only when we go through the Soul's Gate of the fifth chakra. Without pure consciousness and mind, it will be impossible to open its doors.

Sixth Chakra - In-dang

❶ The sixth chakra is located between the eyebrows. Lightly press down on that center point, about a half an inch above your eyebrows, the in-dang point.

❷ Now release the pressure of your fingers. Concentrate on the point just behind them. While feeling the beating of your pulse through the forehead, maintain the sensation of pressure.

❸ Lifting both hands, press down and massage the temples on both sides of your head.

❹ Now release the pressure. Imagine a thin line of energy that connects the two temple points, called *tae-yang* points. Draw a line from the center of the temple line to your sixth chakra.

❺ Form a T-line of energy inside your head. Concentrate on the point of intersection where it bisects the center of your brain. Breathe in and feel the breath enter the third eye. Breathe out and feel the breath exit through the forehead.

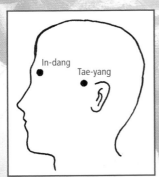

In-dang
Tae-yang

116

Awakening the Soul

A dark blue lotus flower with two leaves represents the sixth chakra. The role of the sixth chakra is to combine with energy from the lower five chakras and elevate it to a higher plane. The energy of the sixth chakra transcends time, integrating past, present, and future into a single moment, the "eternal now." Because of the insights it provides, we refer to it as "the Third Eye." When the sixth chakra is open, one may have insight into the nature of time and the universe, heightened instinct, superior insight, and the ability to give tangible form to imagination.

One with an active and functional sixth chakra immediately sees into the heart of a problem, offering help where it is needed most. With a finger on the pulse of the future, this person will be able to navigate wisely through the present. By contrast, someone with a weak sixth chakra lacks a flow of fresh, creative ideas and cannot easily translate ideas into reality.

One often experiences special abilities when the sixth chakra is active. Just as physical life begins with conception in the womb, spiritual life begins with spiritual conception in the sixth chakra. When the soul awakens, a human can feel genuine love, mercy, and compassion for the Earth and her creatures.

Seventh Chakra - Baek-hwe

❶ Shift your awareness to the top of your head . . . the seventh chakra. As the sixth chakra awakens, the seventh chakra follows soon after.

❷ Maintaining the energy lines from the sixth chakra, connect them to the top of your head. Lightly press down on the crown of your head. Now release the pressure of your fingers. Expand the sensation of the chakra. Feel the vibration that radiates outward from the forehead to the crown of the head.

❸ Now imagine a swirling vortex of energy being drawn into the seventh chakra . . . a solid pillar of energy connecting all of your chakras.

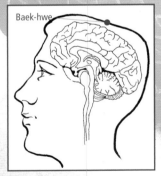

Baek-hwe

Complete Unity of Body, Emotions, and Soul

A thousand-leaf, lavender lotus flower symbolizes the seventh chakra. This chakra symbolizes perfect harmony and complete integration of body, emotion, mind, and spirit. The seventh chakra creates truth and happiness in their purest essence. Here, a sense of the individual self disappears. Awareness is from a place of truth, and everything is in holistic unity, without the illusion of separation. This allows you to fully experience the harmonious order of the cosmos.

An individual with an inactive seventh chakra will not be able to experience spiritual existence, nor to understand the realm of the soul and the universe. Inability to acknowledge the spiritual aspect of life means ignorance of the essential purpose of life.

It is not possible to explain the awakening of the seventh chakra with words. Neither is it possible to analyze it in logical or scientific terms. The seventh chakra is a place of infinity, where suffering caused by illusory pleasure, pain, fame, and wealth is nonexistent. To find your own divinity, to reach a state of salvation, and to reach Nirvana all refer to a full awakening of the seventh chakra.

Activating the Chakras with Vibration

Vibration is the easiest and most effective way of awakening and activating the chakras. It is more efficient to activate the whole chakra system at once through vibration training, rather than activating each chakra one by one. A prerequisite to activating the chakras is the unimpeded and free flow of energy throughout the body. Vibration training is the most effective way of achieving an uninterrupted energy flow. Self-vibration training is an excellent way to activate the first through fourth chakras. Once the four lower chakras are active, the remaining chakras become active just from the power of the lower four.

A sick cell has a different resonant frequency than a healthy cell. In fact, the reason for illness is that cells, or an organ, have lost their natural frequency. Through vibration training, we can recover the lost, natural frequency, and thereby restore health to afflicted areas of the body.

Self-vibration training is like Energy Dance in practice. When you do Energy Dance, the motion occurs spontaneously as you trace the subtle sensation of energy in your hands. Likewise, self-vibration training occurs spontaneously when you stop the flow of conscious thought and apply vibratory stimulation to your body. It is essential that you calm your chattering mind during Vibration Training. During Energy Dance people tend to experience an absence of thoughts, leading to inner peace and joy that arises when following paths of energy. During Vibration Training, you must let yourself go and embrace the natural vibration of life that emanates from deep inside the brain stem.

The primary reason for difficulty with Vibration Training is the inability to let go of inhibition or self-consciousness from the left brain. This separates you from the flow of the universal life force. Only when you let go of your conscious thoughts can you communicate with that universal life force and experience harmony within. Therefore, Healing Chakras training begins with letting go of your chattering mind.

However, when you first begin Vibration Training, some form of conscious effort is necessary to get going. First, stimulate the energy points in the center of the bottom of your feet in order to generate a certain vibration, which will then radiate out to the chakras above. When you feel your body begin to generate a rhythm, let go and immerse yourself in that rhythm with joy and abandon.

In the beginning, play bright, rhythmic music to start the self-vibration process. Once you have developed a naturally occurring rhythm, concentrate only on the movements of your body. Close your eyes and listen to the music. Let the rhythm of the music merge with your own rhythm until you feel your body move with, and then become, the rhythm itself. This is the most comfortable and natural state we can experience.

Beginning Vibration Training

❶ Stand with your feet shoulder width apart, with your arms loose and relaxed along your sides. Let a light smile float upon your face.

❷ With a slight flex of the knees, spring up and down lightly on your toes. Concentrate on your Yong-chun points, located on the bottoms of your feet. Feel the energy of the Earth flow upward through your legs, though your knees. Feel the bottom of your feet. Yong-chun . . . yong-chun . . . yong-chun . . .

❸ Shift your awareness slowly from the bottom of your feet to your ankles. Ankles . . . ankles . . . ankles . . .

❹ Continue moving your body up and down, focusing on the rhythm . . . Moving up and down, feel your muscles working. Knees . . . knees . . . knees . . .

❺ Now focus on your hips. expanding the sensation throughout your legs, until the lower body vibrates with your own unique rhythm.

Yong-chun

Chakra Vibration Training

❶ Touch your tongue lightly to the roof of your mouth. Feel the vibration in your first chakra. The vibration gradually expands upward into the lower abdomen. Concentrate on the second chakra. Feel the vibration in your uterus or bladder.

❷ Awaken the sensation of the second chakra. Move your waist to the front, back, and sides, expanding the vibration.

❸ Feel the energy travel up and down your first and second chakras, moving your whole body up and down. Feel your intestines twist and uncurl as your waist moves around and around. As the second chakra becomes warm, you can feel a stream of cold energy flowing out through your first chakra.

❹ The vibration that began in your tailbone now travels upward to each vertebra of the spine, stimulating and caressing

each one, all the way to your neck. The energy from your head flows down to the first chakra, leaving your head cool and your abdomen warm.

❺ Now concentrate on the third chakra, just above the navel. The energy lying stagnant in the stomach begins to unfurl and move. Stomach . . . liver . . . kidneys . . . Energy is connecting the organs and creating warmth.

❻ Now concentrate on the fourth chakra, your heart chakra. Let the vibration take hold of your arms and shoulders. The energy lying stagnant in the chest flows outward through your palms and fingertips.

❼ Now concentrate on the fifth chakra in your throat. Your head may move from side to side, rotating to the left and right. Let the stagnant energy flow outward through the palms .

❽ Concentrate for two or three minutes on the sensation of each chakra. Feel your lips, tongue, and face. Feel every cell, every organ, every blood vessel vibrate. Feel your whole body tremble with the joy of energy, connecting your body's chakras from your tailbone to the top of your head.

❾ Immerse yourself wholly in the currents of energy and let the energy flow through any blockages. You may feel strong vibration around the blocked areas. Your spine unwinds with the flow and your back straightens. Your head and neck move and rotate freely. Your hands might tap, your chest and all over your body to the joyful rhythm of life's natural resonance being expressed through your body. Your body moves and shakes.

126

Concluding Chakra Vibration Training

❶ Now gradually stop the vibration. Bring your hands with palms up to your lower abdomen.

❷ Slowly bring your right hand up to the seventh chakra while you breathe in. Turn your right hand over so that it faces the ground. As you breathe out, bring it down all the way to your lower abdomen, sweeping down the length of your torso. Repeat this motion three times.

❸ Now sit in half lotus position with your palms facing upward. Breathe in as you bring your hands to chest level. Breathe out as you lower your hands to your lower abdomen once more. Repeat this until you feel your body enter a state of comfortable relaxation. Then lower your hands onto your knees. Conclude the training by internally observing each individual chakra.

Vocal Chakra Healing

Music of all sorts has a dramatic effect on the chakras. If you have ever felt energized through listening to certain music, then you have already experienced this. Any time you like, you can use live or recorded music to help enliven your entire energy system.

You don't have to rely on other people's music, however. You can make your own. Even if you don't think you are a good singer, you can use your voice to help heal your chakras. When you use your own voice, the vibrations will be even more intense because they are coming from within you.

The act of giving voice to inner energy is called "toning." According to Dr. Don Campbell of the American Sound Education Health Research Institute, toning increases oxygen supply and enhances relaxation of the body by facilitating the flow of energy. Sound or voice is a very effective way to slow the flow of thoughts and emotions and create space in which to concentrate on your body, mind, and energy.

Whenever you use your voice, but especially when you sing, you stimulate the body's internal organs and cells with a subtle vibrations of sound waves. The "Om" sound, used by many spiritual traditions, is especially effective for creating balance and harmony among all the internal organs. The sound "Om" has traditionally been the sound of Oneness, symbolizing the essential unity of all things in the universe.

❶ Sit or stand in a comfortable position and relax.

❷ Place your hands in front of your heart in prayer position. Lightly touch your tongue to the roof of your mouth. Close your eyes and give voice to the sound "Om." Elongate the "Om" sound, imagining that you are drawing energy up from the first chakra.

❸ Let the vibration from the first chakra continue through each chakra, arriving at the seventh. Continue making the "Om" sound and feel the subtle vibration in the cells and organs of your body. The vibration becomes stronger, moving your body to the rhythm of your own voice.

❹ Let yourself move to the naturally occurring rhythm, and continue voicing the "Om" sound. Imagine the vibration from your body radiating outward, expanding. Imagine each cell pulsating rhythmically to your voice. The sound of "Om" is ringing throughout the cosmos as you ride the waves, expanding the horizon of your awareness.

❺ Imagine the whole universe filled with vibrations of the sound as you become one with cosmic awareness. Shake joyfully with the vibration of your voice as each chakra blossoms spontaneously. Each chakra, a lotus flower of a different form. Observe your body silently; feel the energy body healthy, happy, and peaceful. Feel your heart as beams of joy and peace radiate outward.

❻ Feel the warm flow from your second chakra. From where does such joy and peace come? This warmth and comfort you feel is the sensation of life. You are meeting life within. This life that exists within you is the real you, existing before the body, alive before your name. Within it, you experience infinite peace.

❼ Now, lower your hands to your knees. Slowly let your awareness float to the surface.

Strengthening the Chakras

The aura is an energy field around our body. It envelops the body fully, and is generated by the chakras. Our aura accurately reflects the state of our body and mind. A weak and hazy aura reflects a malfunctioning chakra system. In a person with a healthy, fully functioning chakra system, the aura is bright and strong.

Surrounding energy affects chakras and aura systems. When standing next to a person who has a healthy chakra system, your own chakras become stronger. On the other hand, standing next to a depressed person may elicit a feeling of depression in you. Very sensitive people can feel a specific part of their body ache when standing next to a person who has pain in the corresponding place.

It is impossible to avoid the influence of surrounding energies in the world. Although you may start out with a healthy chakra system, it can lose harmony due to exposure to unbalanced energy. However, you need not become a hermit in order to maintain a healthy chakra system. To protect the auric field, it is possible to develop a protective energy shield around your body. This allows you to maintain a close relationship with people while, at the same time, purifying and protecting your own energy system. I call this energy shield an energy capsule.

An energy capsule is different from the naturally occurring aura, in that it occurs through conscious awareness and consists of the fundamental vibration of the universe. Imagine that a small, circular hole exists in the energy capsule on top of the head that connects you to a supply of fresh, positive energy from the universe. Directly in front of this column of energy, imagine a smaller hole that pumps negative and stagnant energy out of the body. With this capsule, it is possible to protect and purify yourself while interacting with the world.

Energy capsule training is especially effective when practiced early in the morning and late at night just before you go to sleep. Practicing capsule training before you fall asleep helps you to rest more deeply, and thus to economize on sleeping time. When feeling tired and fatigued during the day, you can recharge yourself by picturing the capsule and consciously receiving energy.

When our chakra system is active and fully functioning, and our spiritual awareness approaches cosmic awareness, our energy body takes on the color of brightly radiating gold. A golden energy body has a powerful loving and healing force, acting to purify negativity. When our awareness becomes one with cosmic awareness, our energy body glows with a whitish silver color of indescribable brightness.

Making an Energy Glove

❶ Raise your hands and gently shake them. Feel the air passing through your fingers, over and under your hands. Continue shaking your hands until you feel a tangible sensation of energy envelop them.

❷ Now, stop shaking your hands. Focus on the energy field, as it forms along the tips of your fingers. Keep concentrating and you will feel electricity or heat on both hands.

❸ Feel the energy flow inward through your fingertips. Focus on the energy flow from your hands to your wrists and elbows all the way up to your shoulders.

❹ Breathe in as you raise both hands, palms facing up, to shoulder level; then lower them again as you exhale. Coordinate the motion of your hands to the rhythm of your breathing. Your hands will move up and down without conscious thinking on your part.

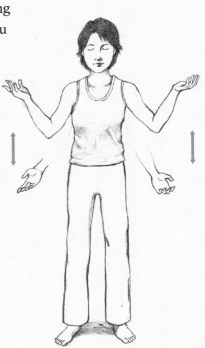

❺ Control your breath with your mind, control your energy with your mind. Your breath will deepen and become slower. Feel the breath from your chest move to your abdomen, then down to your feet, spreading outward in all directions, until it reaches every cell in your body, each cell breathing in and out. This is how your mind moves energy. It is how energy moves the body.

Generating a Capsule of Energy

❶ Keeping the feeling of energy that surrounds your hands, bring your hands close to your face . . .

❷ When your hands are about four inches from your face, wash your face with energy, without touching it, but with the living sensation of warm energy enveloping your face.

❸ Sweep from your face to the back of your head, elongating the energy sheath. Now sweep and cover both arms with this energy sheath. Then sweep from your chest, to your waist, to your legs. You are putting on a veil of energy.

❹ Now imagine a thick, pulsating energy capsule, about eight inches from your skin, surrounding your whole body. Imagine

a small hole on top of your head into which pure silver-white energy flows. In this way, you can fill yourself with energy whenever you wish. Imagine a smaller hole on top of the head from which stagnant energy escapes.

❺ Breathe and feel the energy capsule, cleansing and purifying. Within the energy capsule, your body and mind are restored to their original purity and health.

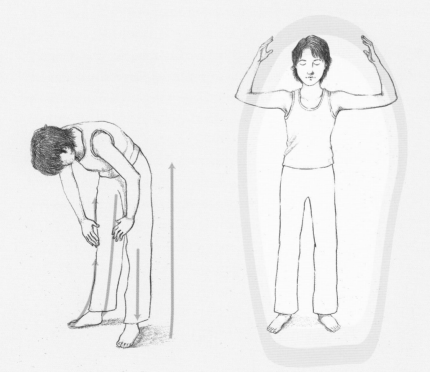

Strengthening the Energy Capsule through Chakra Training

❶ Stand with your legs shoulder width apart with your knees bent at about 15 degrees.

❷ Raise your hands to chest level, as if holding a barrel in your arms. Feel the energy of the Earth travel up to your knees. Energy enters your body through the bottom of your feet, passing through the first chakra and gathering in the second chakra. Through the seventh chakra, you feel a connection to the energy of heaven. The energies of heaven and earth meet in your second chakra.

❸ To strengthen the sensation of energy, imagine a heavy boulder on top of your head. Imagine the ground rising to lift up your feet. Feeling the pressure of heaven and Earth, link the energies from your toes to your head.

❹ Your body stands upright with the strength of heaven and Earth, becoming a passageway for the energy. Focus on your spine and feel a solid pillar of energy that connects your tailbone to your seventh chakra. As you breathe in and out, feel the pillar becoming thicker.

❺ Now, inhale and hold your breath for three to five seconds, feeling the pillar of energy growing thicker. Now breathe out, and feel the energy pillar growing thinner.

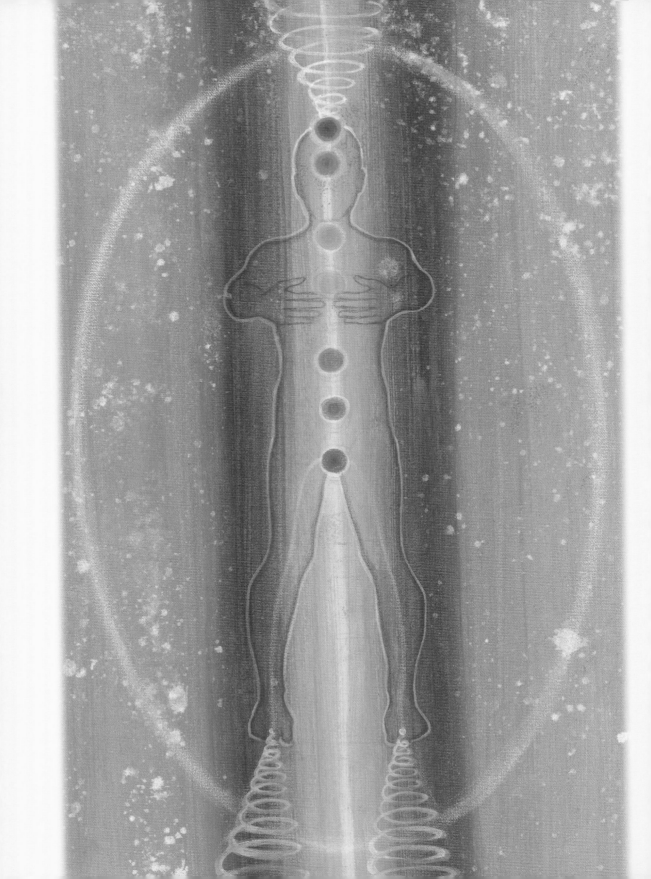

❻ Breathe in again and tighten your sphincter muscle. Feel the energy rise from your tailbone to the top of your head. Hold your breath for a moment. Now breathe out once again, feeling the chakras along your spine. Breathe in and out until you feel the chakras coming alive.

❼ Now, place both hands over the second chakra, about four inches from your skin. Place a field of warm energy over your second chakra. Let the energy of the Earth flow upward through your feet, to your knees, and into your first chakra, turning like a tornado and gathering in your lower abdomen.

❽ Pure energy of the heavens flows in through your seventh chakra and down through your other chakras. The energy from the earth below and the energy from the heavens above meet in your lower abdomen in a swirling of Yin and Yang.

❾ Now, silently feel the warmth of these energies and expand the swirling sensation of energy to envelop all of you, until you palpably feel its presence. As you breathe in and out the energy capsule becomes stronger and brighter.

Healing the Chakras

If only one or some of the seven chakras develop and become active, the whole system becomes unbalanced. A person repeatedly engaged in mental activity while working has a well-developed system of upper chakras. Without working to maintain balance, the person's lower chakras will weaken, increasing susceptibility to depression or other types of mental instability. The lower body will also weaken physically.

Two ways of restoring harmonious balance to the body are through self-healing and healing with a partner. Both methods require the ability to feel the chakras and the energy body. However, it is even possible for beginners to engage in these healing practices.

It is important for a beginner to trust his or her own sensitivity, when he or she practices a partner healing. Take some time to observe your partner, observing his or her energy. Pay attention to the color, temperature, brightness, and clarity of the chakras. Begin to sense the stream of energy coming from the other person.

In the lower three chakras, there is a feeling of warmth from the color red. From the fifth to the seventh chakras, there is a feeling of cool blueness. On the fourth chakra, you can feel a balance of red and blue, in both color and warmth. A problem with the lower chakras transmits as a cold sensation that is white or bluish-black. A problem in the upper chakras presents itself as a hot sensation of dark, angry red. While this may seem difficult at first, with practice and confidence you will be able to read the chakras accurately.

As you place a sheath of energy on another person, you can sense the state of his or her energy body. Problems with the energy body are conveyed by dark or cold sensations, or a sense of hesitation in the formation of the energy capsule. When you feel coldness over a particular part, remove it, and infuse the exact location with warmth. When you find an area of the energy sheath that is thin, infuse that area with more concentrated energy. When you feel stagnant or negative energy, draw the energy out and replace it with fresh, positive energy.

There are two methods of communicating energy to others. One technique entails placing your hand about two inches from the receiver, and moving it back and forth with a rhythmic, spring-like motion. You can also transmit energy by rotating your hand in a clockwise direction—again, keeping your hands two inches from the receiver. Both partners should be in a state of patient receptivity. Purity of intention is necessary for healing. Give energy with love and sincerity. Receive energy with gratitude and trust.

Shower of Light

❶ Close your eyes and stand or sit comfortably with your neck and back straight.

❷ Visualize a bright, golden sun suspended just above your head. Imagine its golden rays showering down on the crown of your head. See the lotus flower of the seventh chakra slowly open its petals, tasting the golden delight of the sun. You may feel a tingling sensation on top of your head as it is bathed by a shower of golden light. Its warmth moves through your body and reaches your first chakra. A clean line of golden energy forms a pillar of light connecting your seven chakras.

❸ Now, imagine the sun shining in front of your face, dazzling, yet soft. Warm and comforting. Feel the light enter your sixth chakra, lighting up your eyes.

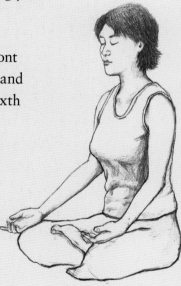

146

❹ Now feel the energy touch upon your fifth chakra, imparting a feeling of warmth to your neck. Move down the chakra ladder. Fourth, third, second, and first. Allow each one to feel the golden light of the sun. Immerse yourself in the field of golden rays, as they cleanse and purify every cell, filling you with the pure energy of the universe.

Transmitting Energy with Your Hands

❶ Bring your hands to your chest, hands two inches apart. Focus on your hands, feeling the field of energy coming alive. Rub your hands together without touching. Feel the energy field becoming stronger.

❷ Place your right hand about four inches from the top of your head. Concentrate on the energy emanating from the seventh chakra. Feel a vortex of golden energy radiating from your hands and spiraling down toward the crown of the head, imparting a feeling of warmth and presence.

❸ Now bring your hand in front of your forehead and transmit energy to your sixth chakra. Feel the gentle tendrils of the energy field reaching out and enveloping you. Now, bring your hands to the sides of your head near your temples and transmit energy.

❹ Lower your hands to your neck, feeling the energy of the fifth chakra. Send blue-green colored energy through your hands. Continue sending the energy until your neck is ringed completely by a collar of blue-green energy.

❺ Come down to the fourth chakra and transmit energy to your chest. If you are having problems with your heart or lungs, or feel a blockage along the front energy pathways, then imagine golden energy reaching out to surround and embrace your heart and lungs.

❻ A problem with the first, second, or third chakras will give the appearance of a white or blackish-red color. Sense the color, light, and temperature of each chakra. If you feel cold, dark strands, pluck them out one by one. If you sense some weakness, then transmit additional energy.

❼ After a while, you will experience a feeling of soft energy flowing to your hands. If you feel an energy blockage in an area, transmit energy as you rotate your hand clockwise, continuing until you break through the barrier, activating and freeing trapped energy.

Partner-Healing

Sensing the Energy Field of a Partner

❶ Stand facing your partner, left palms facing skyward, right palms facing the ground. Bring your hands about two inches away from your partner's palms.

❷ Close your eyes and feel the energy fields of one another . . . hands moving closer together. . . then further apart, continuously strengthening the bond of mutual energy.

❸ Now, one partner lowers his arms and stands in a relaxed position with both hands about two inches from your partner's body. Feel the energy field of different areas of the body, including the shoulders, arms, chest, and legs. Then, begin from the bottom and come back up again, feeling the energy field of your partner's back. Repeat this three times, until you have a clear sense of the energy field that surrounds your partner. Focus on the subtle vibration of energy that you can sense with your fingertips.

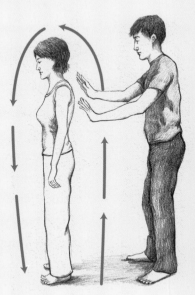

❹ Discuss the condition of the energy field with your partner.

Putting an Energy Capsule on a Partner

❶ First, rub your hands together to gather energy.

❷ Standing about ten inches from your partner, surround your partner with a capsule of energy.

❸ Using the energy of your hands, begin with the face. Move down the front and up the back of your partner as before.

❹ This time, instead of just feeling the energy, place a sheath of energy over your partner. Wrap a capsule of healing energy around your partner, from top to bottom.

❺ Concentrate on your partner's individual chakras throughout this process. You may feel a cool draft or a stream of warmth. Coolness signifies lack of circulation and may create a prickling sensation in your hands. In some areas, you may feel a thick stream or lump of energy. In other areas, energy may be subtle and barely perceptible.

❻ Certain areas may resist developing a capsule and create a sensation of dissolving the energy. Focus your energy on these areas and pass your hands over them repeatedly. Trust your energy sensitivity, instinct, and insight to move your hands, stopping the flow of thoughts, intellect, and judgment.

❼ Once you completely trust in your ability to sense energy, your hands will move of their own accord. They will find weak and painful spots and will reinforce areas in need of energy. Let your hands be guided by the sensation of energy.

❽ Sweeping downward from the top of the head, focus on the sensation of the seventh, sixth, and fifth chakras. If you sense darkness or coolness in the fifth chakra, there may be a problem with the thyroid glands. Draw the stream of coolness out of the neck as if you were pulling on a thread. Then replenish it with fresh energy.

❾ When you perceive a sense of balance in the area, move down to the next chakra. Feel the state of the fourth chakra with your hands. If you sense coolness, darkness, or prickling, draw the negative energies out with your hands.

❿ When working on the third chakra or below, bend your knees so that you are comfortable. Sense the temperature of the first and second chakras. If you feel a cool draft, counter it with a blast of warm energy from your hands until you feel the area covered with warmth.

⓫ Repeat the motions of this chakra healing three times. You will feel the energy field become stronger and purer each time you pass over your partner's body.

⓬ Afterward, briskly sweep down the whole body. With your partner, discuss what each of you felt during the process. Through this, your sensitivity to energy will increase and your healing powers will be enhanced.

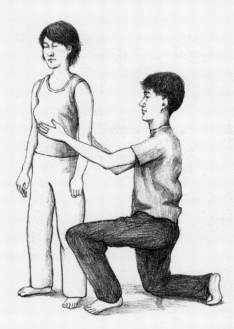

Chakra Meditation

There are many kinds of meditation in the world, but all of them help to quiet the mind. This benefit is part of what makes meditation so healthy—it can help us to quiet our chattering minds for deep relaxation and better focus.

Chakra meditation is designed to bring you back to neutrality, to a place of balance. You might call this "zero point," a place where you can begin again with a fresh, new mind. This is very important for the health of the chakras because it helps us to move past any mental and spiritual issues that may be affecting them.

By practicing to return to this "zero point," you are essentially training yourself to listen to your own soul. As your mind's constant internal chatter is silenced, you will be more able to commune directly with your own soul.

Most people live out their lives without communicating with their soul. Emotions, thoughts, preconceptions . . . these things are not your soul. Yet, many people mistake these things for their soul. Throughout our lives, we are bombarded with an endless stream of information that prevents our souls from being free. Our dislikes, as well as our desires, cage our souls.

Your soul's freedom begins the moment you step away from limitations of your conscious mind. Just for this moment, let go of all thoughts, preconceptions, and emotions. Let your body move according to the flow of energy. Then you will hear the voice of your soul.

Listening to the Message of the Soul

❶ Sit in half lotus position and close your eyes.

❷ Imagine a single lotus flower as it takes root in your body and blossoms forth. Imagine the stalk of the lotus rising along your spine, its roots embedded in the first chakra. The bud of the lotus flower lies softly on top of the seventh chakra.

❸ As you breathe in, let your consciousness travel from the root of the lotus flower to the bud of the lotus flower.

❹ As you breathe out, let your consciousness travel downward to the first chakra. Let the flower return to a bud while breathing in and blossom forth again as you breathe out.

❺ As your breathing deepens, the flower opens wide, its roots extending in all directions. As the flower blossoms, your soul blooms beautifully, communicating freely with cosmic energy. Listen to the message of the cosmos coming through the beauty of the lotus flower.

❻ Now, with both hands, envelop the sixth chakra. A golden light is seeping through your sixth chakra, Heaven's Palace. Energy emanating from your hands is going into the cells deep inside your brain. It softly soothes the brain stem, awakening the pure soul sleeping therein. Meet the light of life that existed before your name in the palace of the sixth chakra.

❼ Say to yourself, "I am eternal, without beginning or end. I am pure love and compassion. I am healthy and I am complete."

❽ Expel fear, doubt, hatred, attachment. Draw out all of these energies. Brighten your sixth chakra with a silvery-white light, translucent and beautiful.

⑨ Now imagine the cosmic energy connecting the sixth and seventh chakras, as the brightly shining Big Dipper, a symbol of the seven chakras and human completion, descends into your sixth and seventh chakras.

⑩ Imagine your soul assuming the shape of a pure white bird and fly from the lotus flower of the seventh chakra.

⑪ Freed from the bars of preconceptions and attachment, fly away into the blue sky. Your soul exists with true freedom in the infinite space of the cosmos. Breathe in and out three times and raise your awareness slowly to the surface.

Pure Consciousness Meditation

This training is to bring separated divinity back to the original oneness. Through the process of meditation, you will bring together body and mind, logic and emotion, False Self and True Self, and all other forms of duality. As you meditate in this position, your breath will deepen naturally and your body will be replenished with energy.

Touch your fingertips together. Since all energy channels of the body are connected through the fingertips, this brings all energies of the organs and chakras together. The place of emptiness is the place where duality no longer exists. This is the place of pure consciousness where cleansing and purification occur. This meditation will return you to yourself, beyond all space and time. This meditation will allow you to meet with the essence of life before it had a name. You may practice this meditation in any comfortable position, sitting or standing.

❶ Concentrate on your lower abdomen, with your back straight and shoulders relaxed.

❷ Bring your fingertips together in front of your chest and form them into a ball. Through the fingertips, all organs are connected and all chakras are bonded. Current flows through your fingertips and warmth greets each finger.

❸ Your mind is truly at rest as golden light fills your hands. Imagine a miniature version of you hidden within the light. You are there, inside the golden aura of the cosmos.

❹ Observe yourself floating in space, pure and unadulterated as at birth. neither man nor woman, without name or title, just pure life. You are infinitely peaceful, within a space inviolable to all, a space of pure consciousness. From this place of pure consciousness, body and mind find harmony and all memories of suffering dissolve, returning you to the zero point.

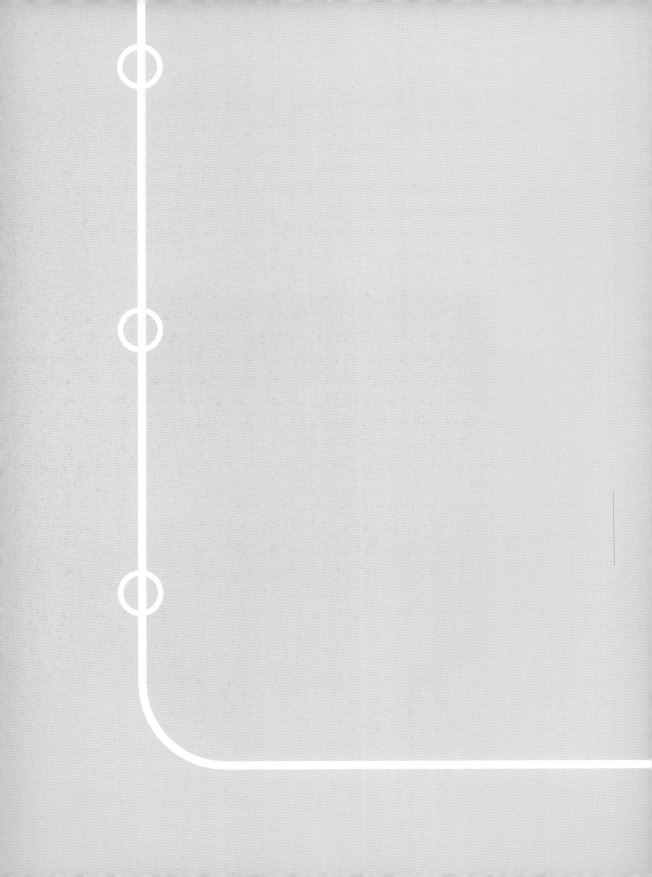

Part V

Living a Healthy
Chakra Lifestyle

Chakra Color Meditation

Every color has its own unique frequency and energy. Psychological and physical responses to different colors are already the subject of much study, with some colors being used for healing purposes. The colors of the chakras incorporate the spectrum of the rainbow, making it virtually impossible to define a specific, definite color for one chakra. The actual colors sensed during your chakra meditation and exercise will vary among individuals. This is why books or meditation groups differ in their choice of colors of the chakras.

Passion, creation, life, love, peace, wisdom, and completion . . . these energies are essential to living. By meditating on these words and concepts every day, you can create happiness and joy. You can be reborn every day with renewed body and mind. It is the energy of your mind and consciousness that heals you. For your mind and consciousness are the mind and consciousness of the cosmos. "My Energy is Cosmic Energy. My Mind is Cosmic Mind." This is what I shouted at the moment of enlightenment. This is truth as I have experienced it.

When you are at a crossroads, when you feel down or lacking in energy. . . when you feel confused and chaotic. . . when you need the power of the cosmos. . . just reach out with your hand, and in return, you will receive health of body and mind.

Chakra Color Meditation is a training method designed to awaken the infinite potential of the brain by activating the chakras through color. We will use the unique vibration of each color to stimulate each individual chakra, which in turn stimulates the brain. When engaging in Chakra Brain Respiration, you can choose a color according to your condition. You can choose a different color for each day of the week, since there are seven to choose from. You will then feel your body and mind filled with energy.

❶ Sit in a comfortable position and relax your body. Choose the color and chakra you want for the day. Find the appropriate picture on pages 22–49. Observe the picture calmly and silently, feeling the sensation of the color . . . cold, hot, warm . . . comfortable . . . energizing . . . soothing . . .

❷ Now, close your eyes and imagine the picture you've just seen. Let the picture become larger and brighter in your mind's eye, infusing your whole being with its light. Let the light cascade over you, allowing the light to be absorbed by your body, exploding in intensity as it hits the corresponding chakra. If you want passion in your life, repeat the words, "Passion . . . passion . . ." as you visualize the color red. Feel the sensation of the particular frequency of vibration that corresponds to the color you have chosen.

❸ Now, breathe the color in and breathe out. Accept the color as you breathe it in, and then expel all the negative energy from the chakra as you breathe out. Imagine the color infusing every crevice and pore of your body, pushing away any negativity.

1 First Chakra: Light of Passion

Bright, solid red symbolizes strength of life force energy. Red is also the color of the Earth, which is the source of all other Earth energies. Focus on the first chakra and commune with her energy for the strength to forgive and the will to be courageous. You will acknowledge and love yourself, with overwhelming passion for life. This passion will make you shine brightly in this reality.

❶ Passion . . . courage . . . strength . . . decisiveness . . . forgiveness . . . Call forth these fundamental energies to the first chakra. Feel the energies seep into your being.

❷ Say to yourself, "I live life with a passion. I have courage and strength. I am decisive and forgiving."

❸ Breathe in . . . and out . . . concentrating on the perineum. Breathe in, and the red energy comes into you through the first chakra. Breathe out, and the red energy goes out through the first chakra. With the breath, you feel crimson energy enveloping your body.

❹ Say to yourself, "A red rose rises through me, a wave of red energy, cresting within my soul."

2   Second Chakra: Light of Creation

Ordinarily we don's make the connection between sexual energy and creativity. However, the energies of the second chakra, when nurtured and developed harmoniously, fuel creativity. One who has an active second chakra is vigorous, sensitive and has a strong sense of aesthetics. On the other hand, diminished second chakra activity will lead to the sense that life is mundane, boring, and meaningless. Creativity is not the unique gift of artists. It is the God-given right of all. All human beings have a divine purpose for being on Earth. It is up to you to find yours. When you meet with the Creator within, you will find your purpose and be free. When you seek to draw from the reservoir of creativity in yourself, focus on the second chakra.

❶ Creativity . . . joy . . . happiness . . . vigor . . . Call forth the scarlet energy to your second chakra, the lower abdomen.

❷ Say to yourself, "I am overflowing with the inner power of creation. I am the creator of my life."

❸ Imagine the sky above with the indescribable beauty of the rising sun as it comes over the horizon, bearing the gift of light, everchanging and exquisite . . . breathe in . . . and breathe out.

❹ Concentrate on your lower abdomen. Feel scarlet energy in the air around you as it becomes part of your energy body. Say, "I am overflowing with creativity. I realize that I am truly the creator of my own life. Joy and happiness flow from me."

3   Third Chakra: Light of Life

The orange of the third chakra calls forth desire and passion for your life's work. The third chakra has the strength to control impulse and habit, giving you an opportunity to change them. If you want to stop smoking or are on a weight loss program, then concentrate on the third chakra. Lack of third chakra activity will lower the level and duration of your ability to concentrate, leaving you vulnerable to diversions. You may also feel frustrated with the lack of progress in the tasks that you do.

❶ Passion for life . . . will . . . action . . . concentration . . .

❷ Call orange energy to your navel.

❸ As you breathe in . . . and out . . .feel the clear exuberance of orange melting away pain, suffering, and indifference.

❹ Feel the energy of courage, hope, and comfort flowing through you. Say to yourself, "I love my work and my life. I am healthy and vital, and filled with energy. I live in this moment, in the very now. Filled with the heat of energy, I feel the dazzling light of life shining through me."

Golden yellow energy has the power to restore balance to the heart and mind. It is the color of forgiveness, understanding, love, and compassion. Overflowing with sympathy, affection, kindness, and hatred, the fourth chakra can very easily become tired and worn, for this chakra has overwhelming power to absorb everything that surrounds it. The fourth chakra's golden light restores strength and peace very quickly. With use of this chakra, it becomes easier to be convincing, as it imparts power to "move" other people's minds. The fourth chakra creates a sense of "we" rather than "I" when dealing with others. If you wish to restore a relationship, focus on the fourth chakra and envelop your heart with its golden light. When you feel that your heart overflows with bright, warm light, imagine yourself reconnecting with the other person.

❶ Understanding . . . love . . . compassion . . . kindness . . . Visualize a field of yellow flowers swaying as one in the breeze.

❷ Powerful golden energy pierces your chest, and fills your heart, lungs, and blood with a golden aura.

❸ Say to yourself, "I am becoming stronger and stronger. I am filled with the power to melt away sadness, loneliness, and hatred, in the powerful gentle strength of the golden light. My heart radiates golden energy to the whole world."

5   Fifth Chakra: Light of Peace

Blue-green color represents inspiration, devotion, peace, and silence. Blue-green is also the color of healing, and the restoration of harmony and balance. Blue-green color has the ability to restore the balance of mind and body. It also helps rid the body of toxins and addictions. When you visualize the blue-green sea or sky, or the color of an emerald, you will feel a calm healing sensation throughout your body. Blue-green also has an ameliorating effect on headaches, anxiety, nervousness, insomnia, and palpitations.

❶ Peace . . . harmony . . . balance . . . healing . . . calmness . . . Imagine a sky without end, so blue and so high. Imagine a sea without depth, so green and so deep.

❷ Say to yourself, "Blue-green energy flows through my neck, sounding the voice of my soul, soft, deep, and powerful. It fills me with peace that remains still and eternal, harmonious and balanced. In harmony, all will complete the healing journey. I am connected with the very center of the universe."

6 Sixth Chakra: **Light of Wisdom**

The sixth chakra is related to insight and intuition. Insight is not a product of intellect, but rather is the wisdom gained from an understanding of the fundamental truths about life. By silencing your thoughts and preparing your mind, you will be able to meet with the light of the sixth chakra that connects to the reservoir of wisdom within. The navy-blue color of the sixth chakra will help you expand your awareness and throw off the yoke of fear and repressed emotions. It has a positive effect on diseases of the eyes and ears. It also has an anesthetizing effect. Deep navy-blue will help you expand your awareness, develop intuition and insight, and offer the gift of inspiration.

❶ Insight . . . intuition . . . wisdom . . . inspiration . . .
The deep, fathomless ocean of wisdom lies within your sixth chakra.

❷ Feel your body disappear into the silent peace of the deep sea. Let your body float into the cosmic ocean, tethered to your soul with a line of dark-blue energy.

❸ Say to yourself, "I inhale the light of wisdom, truth, and divinity. I exhale with inspiration, intuition, and insight. I can hear the voice of wisdom within. I can feel the breath of Truth. I can breathe the light of divinity."

7 Seventh Chakra: **Light of Completion**

The seventh chakra is the place where all that has been previously separated comes together in Oneness. You and me . . . life and death . . . mind and body . . . man and woman . . . all of these melt into the large pot of life. With unshakable trust in our own divinity, we experience our eternal nature. When we realize our own divinity, we also recognize that fear, loneliness, and other emotions are illusions. Once we rip open the curtain of illusions, we will receive dazzling inspiration and insight. The light of the seventh chakra will lead us to that place of completion, the place of cosmic divinity. The lavender light of the seventh chakra symbolizes respect for life and the sacredness of life.

❶ Completion . . . Oneness . . . freedom of soul . . . Whenever you wish, you can will this lavender light to enter you through the crown of your head.

❷ Say to yourself, "All-knowing and filled with original completeness, I am perfect and complete and embraced by the light. I am neither man nor woman. I am neither good nor evil. I am eternal and free. As I breathe in . . . and out . . . All the separateness I feel becomes one."

2. Exercises to Awaken the Chakras

Chakra exercises are designed to facilitate the flow of energy throughout the body by stimulating each chakra and associated energy channels. The following exercises help you locate, consciously feel, and awaken the individual chakras.

First Chakra ## Strength, courage, and decisiveness

【Sphincter Muscle Contraction/Relaxation Exercise】

❶ Stand with your legs shoulder width apart and bring your knees together, leaving a space the size of a fist between your knees. Raise your arms straight out in front of you. Straighten your back and hips.

❷ As you breathe in, expand your abdomen and bring your thighs toward the middle while tightening your sphincter muscle. At the same time, make your hands into fists. Then pause.

❸ Breathe out, while you relax your sphincter muscle and pull your abdomen in. Repeat this exercise for ten minutes in the morning and evening.

【 Exercise to Stimulate the Perineum 】

❶ Sit in a butterfly position and grab
your ankles with both hands.

❷ Raise your hips up and down so
that your first chakra area is
stimulated. Repeat ten times.

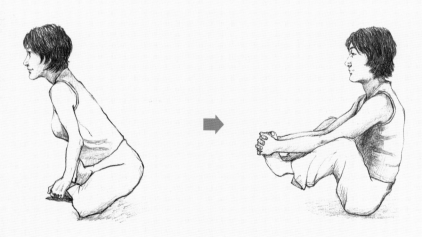

When seeking creativity

【 Exercise to Stimulate the Lower Abdomen and Kidneys 】

❶ Lie on your stomach with your arms to the sides. Point your toes. Raise your right leg straight up without bending your knees as you breathe in. Then, lower your leg slowly as you breathe out. Repeat this with your left leg.

❷ Once you are accustomed to the exercise, repeat the above motion with both legs at the same time.

【 Exercise to Strengthen the Lower Abdomen 】

❶ Lie flat on your back. Place your hands behind your head and interlock your fingers. Raise your knees and bring your heels toward your hips.

❷ Breathe in and raise your back up, bringing your knees together and tightening your hips.

❸ Breathe out and lower your back. Repeat this motion three times.

Inner will and desire

【 Exercise to Strengthen the Stomach 】

❶ Sit in half lotus position with your right leg on top and place your right hand on top of your right foot. Breathe in and raise your left arm skyward while looking at the back of your left hand.

❷ Lower your hand as your breathe out. Repeat with the other hand. Continue for ten minutes.

【 Exercise to Strengthen the Internal Organs 】

① Lie on your stomach and raise your upper body by pushing up with your arms. With your toes pushing against the floor, breathe in and pull your upper body up and back as far as it will go. As you breathe out, relax.

② This time, as you breathe in, tighten your whole body, including your toes until they are off the ground. Breathe out and relax. Raising your legs just a little bit stimulates your digestive organs a great deal.

③ When doing this exercise, concentrate on the parts of your body that are being worked, including your abdominal area and legs. This exercise stretches the front abdominal and quadriceps areas, stimulating the energy channels related to digestion. Repeat 6–8 times every day.

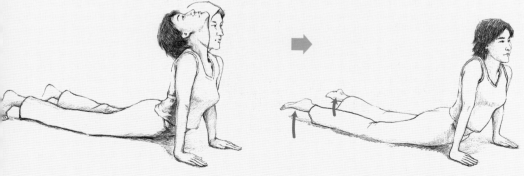

Relief from anxiety and nervousness

【 Exercise to Expand the Chest 】

❶ Bring your hands together in front of your chest and make them into fists.

❷ As you breathe in, pull your arms back and expand your chest as much as possible. Keep your head back slightly and your back straight, with a slight tightening of your shoulders and chest. Pause for 10 seconds.

❸ Breathe out and bring your hands together in front of your chest again as you bend forward a little. Repeat this motion 10 times. This exercise will bring a refreshing feeling to your chest and shoulders, while relieving stress. You will also feel your mind recover comfort and peace.

【 Exercise to Strengthen the Lungs 】

❶ Stand with your legs wide open, knees slightly bent, and lift your arms toward the sky, palms facing upward.

❷ Straighten your back, spine, and chest. Tighten your chest and shoulder muscles as you breathe naturally. In the beginning, hold this position for 3 minutes, then expand the time to 5–20 minutes. This exercise helps you to increase the flow of energy to your lungs by stimulating the relevant points on the spine.

Emotional control and inner peace

【 Exercise to Open the Throat 】

❶ With your hands on your thighs, step one leg forward and the other leg back. Your front leg should be bent at the knee, the back leg straight.

❷ Breathe in as you tilt your head backward, stretching your neck.

❸ Breathe out and bring your head back to its original position. Repeat this motion three times. Also try this with your legs switched.

【 Exercise to Open the Throat 】

❶ Kneel with your hips resting on your heels. Place both hands on your back, approximately where your kidneys are located.

❷ Breathe in and bend your upper body backward as much as possible.

❸ Breathe out and bend your back and head forward. Pull your chin down so that it touches your chest.

Intuition, inspiration, and insight

【 **Exercise to Awaken the "Third Eye"** 】

❶ Stand with your legs spread wide and bend your knees about 15 degrees.

❷ Make a triangle by touching your thumbs and index fingers and place it over your "third eye" point in your forehead. Breathing naturally, visualize the energy of the sun entering through the triangle into your forehead. Direct your gaze about 15 degrees skyward. Continue for 5 minutes.

【 **Exercise to Stimulate the Temples** 】

❶ Sit comfortably with your eyes closed. Bring one open hand up close to your temple. Allow the flow of energy to travel from your hand to your temple.

❷ The other hand should be at the center of your lower back, with the middle finger and the thumb touching in a loop. Imagine breathing through the back of the third chakra. The thumb is connected to your second chakra energy, while the middle finger is connected to your sixth chakra energy. The loop facilitates intermingling of the energies.

Oneness with the Cosmos

【 Pyramid Position 】

❶ Bring the five fingers of each hand together to form a pyramidlike shape. The pyramid represents a very stable form of energy. Place the pyramid shape on top of your head. Raise your chin about 15 degrees skyward.

❷ Kneel with your knees touching, back straight, and your feet overlapping. If overlapping the entire foot is difficult, just overlap the big toes.

❸ Breathe naturally for 3–5 minutes and feel the flow of energy throughout your body.

【 Lotus Position 】

❶ Sit comfortably in half lotus position and focus on your mind. Raise both hands and gradually bring them to your forehead, leaving a little space in between. Focus on the feeling that comes alive between your hands.

❷ Slowly expand and contract the space between your hands. Imagine your hands as a lotus flower, petals blossoming when you pull your hands apart, and contracting into a bud when you bring your hands together again.

❸ Breathe slowly, as you sweep down with your hands from your head to your lower abdomen. Focus on your lower abdomen and continue with the meditation.

Living a Healthy Chakra Lifestyle 185

Index

1st chakra, 23–25, 87, 106–107, 165
2nd chakra, 27–29, 89, 108–109, 166, 174–175
3d chakra, 31–33, 111–112, 167, 176–177
4th chakra, 35–37, 89, 112–113, 168, 178–179
5th chakra, 39–41, 87–88, 170, 172–173, 180–181
6th chakra, 43–45, 89, 170, 182–183
7th chakra, 47–49, 88, 171, 184–185
acceptance, 37
authority, 32
brain stem, 61
brain, 58–61
Chun–bu–kyung, 71–86
confidence, 24
consciousness, 57, 158–59
cosmic energy, 48–49
creativity, 32–33
crown chakra, see seventh chakra
divinity, 37, 41, 48, 72, 74–75
Earth palace, 89–90
Earth Palace, see second chakra
Earth, 28
emotions, 28–29, 36–37
empowerment, 32
energy body, 54–55
energy, 18–21, 66–67, 96–97
enlightenment, 11–15, 49, 72
essence, 158–159
fatigue, 28
fifth chakra, 39–41, 87–88, 170, 172–173, 180–181
first chakra, 23–25, 87, 106–107, 165
fourth chakra, 35–37, 89, 112–113, 168, 178–179
Great Universe, 67
heart blockage, 36
heart chakra, see fourth chakra
heaven, 48–29
Heaven's Gate, see seventh chakra

Heaven's Palace, see sixth chakra
Heavenly Code, see Chun–bu–kyung
infancy, 24
information, 45
intellect, 44
intuition, 44
Jade Gate, see first chakra
ki, see energy
life purpose, 45
limbic system, 61
Mind Palace, see fourth chakra
neo-cortex, 61
oneness, 90, 158–159, 184
parents, 24
purification, 158–159
rational mind, 44–45
root chakra, see first chakra
sacral chakra, see second chakra
second chakra, 27–29, 89, 108–109, 166, 174–175
self-preservation, 24
seventh chakra, 47–49, 88, 171, 184–185
sex, 24
Shin-sun-do, 12–13, 66–69, 90
shyness, 40
sixth chakra, 43–45, 89, 170, 182–183
Small Universe, 67
solar plexus, see third chakra
soul, 39–41, 48, 74–75, 90–93
Soul's Gate, see fifth chakra
spiritual body, 54–55
Sun Lotus, see third chakra
third chakra, 31–33, 111–112, 167, 176–177
third eye, see sixth chakra
Three Births, 90
three gates, 87–88
throat chakra, see fifth chakra
triad of heaven, Earth, and human, 48, 71
True Self, 36, 75
vibration, 62–63,
water up, fire down, 28, 45, 109

Earth Citizen: Recovering Our Humanity
Ilchi Lee

Ilchi Lee's new book, *Earth Citizen*, is humanity's passport to a whole new world. In the book, Lee contends that while the cultures of the world may remain diverse, we are all united by our dependence on a single planet—the Earth. It is only by realizing our common humanity through the Earth that we can come together as one to create a peaceful and sustainable way of life on the planet.

Paperback
US $7.95
ISBN-13: 9781935127253

Brain Wave Vibration: Getting Back into the Rhythm of a Happy, Healthy Life
Ilchi Lee

Brain Wave Vibration is a powerful, easy-to-follow brain fitness and holistic healing method that helps people bring their bodies and minds back into balance for total health, happiness, and peace. Through this book, author Ilchi Lee teaches this simple truth: Creating a miracle is just a matter of coming back to who you really are. More than a physical training technique, Brain Wave Vibration is a call to action, a plea to uncover the vast abilities that lie within your brain.

Paperback
US $14.00
ISBN-13: 9781935127000

Home Healing Massage: Hwal-gong for Everyday Wellness
Institute of Human Technology

Home Healing Massage is a comprehensive guide to the natural healing power of touch. Based on ancient Korean massage techniques, these methods will give you increased ability to develop total wellness for yourself and your entire family. Each fully illustrated chapter provides a complete overview of basic Asian energy principles and massage techniques that effectively alleviate many ailments common in today's world, including stress and pain. Most of all, you will be able to experience the sheer joy of giving and receiving love through the act of hands-on healing.

Paperback
US $27.95
ISBN-13: 9781935127024

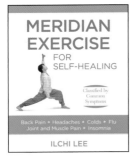

Meridian Exercise for Self-Healing
Ilchi Lee

This full-color, user-friendly book identifies specific meridian exercises to alleviate common ailments, including headache, stress, colds, and flu, as well as more serious conditions, such as high blood pressure, diabetes, and thyroid disorders. Meridian exercise is a technique developed and perfected over the course of thousands of years in the Asian holistic healing traditions. Ilchi Lee's book translates these ancient techniques for the modern human.

Paperback
US $29.95
ISBN-13: 9781935127109

Power of the Chun Bu Kyung
Ilchi Lee

This CD features various versions of the Chun Bu Kyung chanted by Ilchi Lee and Dahn masters of the Sedona Mago Retreat Center. It is ideal for your morning and evening routine, and for centering, healing, and finding peace in meditation. Also available as a digital download from www.bestlifemedia.com.

Audio CD
US $19.95
ISBN-13: 9781935127062

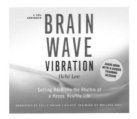

Brain Wave Vibration: Audio Book with a Guided Training Session
Ilchi Lee

Catch the wave of the powerful brain fitness training that has already transformed thousands of lives. This audio presentation of Brain Wave Vibration provides tips for practice and a complete, easy-to-follow training session, as well as profound insights into the nature of human happiness and fulfillment. Now available for download at www.bestlifemedia.com.

Audio book
US $24.95
ISBN-13: 9781935127079

Dahn Yoga Essentials: Featuring Brain Wave Vibration
With Dawn Quaresima

Develop a strong and flexible body, boost your energy and vitality, and bring balance back into your life with the newest Dahn Yoga DVD. Certified Dahn Yoga instructor Dawn Quaresima guides you through a one-hour training session that includes deep stretching exercises, meditative breathing techniques, and energy awareness meditation. On additional tracks she leads you through the only video presentations available of Brain Wave Vibration, a simple and effective stress-relieving moving meditation, and Dahn Yoga Energy Breathing, five breathing postures for restoring your vitality.

US $19.95
DVD
ISBN-13: 9781935127260

Healing Chakras Wall Art
Art by Al Choi

This wall art of the seven chakras is not just a beautiful hanging decoration, but a meditation tool for chakra balancing and healing. The chakras are the seven key energy centers of our body. Each chakra has unique characteristics and all are closely connected to the state of our mind, body, and spirit. Hang this wall art featuring vibrant chakra colors in any room and look at it while doing chakra meditations. It will help you awaken and balance your chakras deeply. Each chakra art was originally hand-painted by artist Al Choi. 6'x40'

Hanging Banner
US $48.00
ISBN-13: 9780979938870

www.bestlifemedia.com

If you would like to learn more about our products, please visit our website, www.bestlifemedia.com. Here you may browse through our books, DVDs, and CDs to find exactly the right match for your personal growth and fulfillment.

About Ilchi Lee

Ilchi Lee was born in 1950 into a Korea embroiled in the upheaval of the Korean War. From a very early age, he questioned the true meaning and purpose of his life. In his youth he was plagued by a restlessness that he could only pacify through intense martial arts training. Eventually, he graduated from college, opened a successful health clinic, and began to raise a family. On the surface, he seemed to be living an ideal life, yet the yearning to understand life on a deeper level would not subside.

In his early thirties, determined to come to terms with his place in the universe, he set off alone into the mountains to undergo twenty-one days of rigorous ascetic training. It was through this training that he realized the ultimate oneness of all things and his calling to live for the benefit of humanity.

When he returned from the mountains, he sought to reach out to people by offering free exercise classes in a local park. At first only one man came, a stroke victim who quickly improved through the exercises, which were based on ancient Korean mind-body training techniques. Hearing about the man's recovery, more and more people gathered in the park to follow Lee's classes. Eventually, inclement weather necessitated the opening of the first Dahn Yoga Center in South Korea.

Dahn Yoga Centers soon opened all across South Korea, and then, in 1986, the first Dahn Center opened in the United States. Additional centers soon followed, which resulted in a network of centers throughout the world. During the intervening years, Lee continued to develop and refine his training techniques. Realizing that the brain is the key to the development of human consciousness, he now combines traditional techniques with various brain development methods, collectively known as Brain Education System Training (BEST). Currently, he serves as president of both the Korea Institute of Brain Science (KIBS) and the International Brain Education Association (IBREA).

Today, Ilchi Lee's movement for health, happiness, and peace continues to grow, taking on many different forms. In addition to Dahn Center activities, many other programs are now available through schools, community colleges, senior centers, and many more venues. Students of Ilchi Lee's BEST training programs are now reaching out to the world in very much the same way that he did when he first started with the man in the park so many years ago.

Please visit www.ilchi.com for more information.

How to use the Healing Chakras Self-Training CD

The Healing Chakra CD is for individual use, with one training session per track. You may choose to train by completing one track per session, or you may prefer to complete the whole CD training in one session. This will take about forty minutes. It is a good idea to read and become familiar with the contents of the main *Healing Chakras* book beforehand.

Tracks 1 and 5 consist of Healing Chakras messages by Ilchi Lee, the creator of Healing Chakras training, recorded in his own voice.

Track 2, "Feeling Your Chakras," is designed to help you identify the exact locations of the chakras. Following this, you will use the power of music, from the flute, drum, harp and other instruments, to expand the sensation.

Track 3, "Activating the Chakras," is an exercise to help you activate and awaken the seven chakras through self-vibration meditation.

Track 4, "Purifying the Chakras," is an exercise to help you cleanse and strengthen your chakra system. Through the flute music, performed by Ilchi Lee himself, you can purify and strengthen the chakras one by one. In an impromptu performance, author and musician Ilchi Lee creates music while riding on a wave of the rhythm of the universe. The result is a powerful healing and soothing effect on the listener. (Instruments used: Indian flute, Native American drums, autoharp, vibratone, and rain stick.)